SALLY CLARKE

30

INGREDIENTS

SALLY CLARKE

30

INGREDIENTS

APRICOT, ASPARAGUS, AUBERGINE
BASIL, BEETROOT, BROAD BEAN, CEP
CHERRY, CHICORY, CLEMENTINE
COBNUT, FENNEL, FIG, LANDCRESS
LEEK, LEMON AND LIME, OLIVE
BLOOD ORANGE, PEA, PEACH, PINE
NUT, POTATO, QUINCE, RASPBERRY
ROCKET, SAGE, SQUASH & PUMPKIN
STRAWBERRY, SWEETCORN, TOMATO

F

FRANCES LINCOLN LIMITED
PUBLISHERS

for Samuel, again

Also by Sally Clarke: *Sally Clarke's Book: Recipes from a restaurant, shop and bakery*

CLARKE'S RESTAURANT
124 Kensington Church Street, London W8 4BH 020 7221 9225 restaurant@sallyclarke.com
Breakfast Monday to Saturday 8 am to 11 am, Lunch Monday to Friday from 12.30 pm
Lunch Saturday from 12 pm, Dinner Monday to Saturday 6.30 pm to 10 pm

SALLY CLARKE SHOP
1 Campden Street, London W8 7EP 020 7229 2190 shop@sallyclarke.com
Monday to Friday 8 am to 8 pm, Saturday 8 am to 5 pm, Sunday 10 am to 4 pm

SALLY CLARKE BAKERY (WHOLESALE)
020 7042 7987 bakery@sallyclarke.com

www.sallyclarke.com   Twitter: @SallyClarkeLtd

BAR ROOM

1

APRICOT

24 *Apricot salad with mozzarella and Marcona almonds*

25 *Almond and apricot kernel ice cream*

27 *Apricots baked with vanilla, cinnamon and lavender*

29 *Croquant d'amande*

2

ASPARAGUS

32 *Asparagus fritters with lemon slices and chive mayonnaise*

35 *White asparagus with poached egg, red wine vinegar and sourdough toast*

37 *Asparagus risotto with spelt, goat cheese and Prosecco*

3

AUBERGINE

40 *Baba ganoush – smoked aubergine with home-made pitta bread*

43 *Baked aubergine, courgette and tomato with ricotta*

45 *Caponata*

4

BASIL

51 *Roasted chicken with basil*

53 *Pale aubergine baked with basil, goat curd and lemon*

54 *Basil ice cream with sugared basil leaves, lemon and black pepper wafers*

5

BEETROOT

58 *Roasted beetroot soup with dill, Bramley apple and soured cream*

61 *Russian salad – beetroot with potato, turnip, carrots and peas*

63 *Baked beetroot and carrots with new season garlic*

6

BROAD BEAN

68 *Broad bean crostini with lemon, olive oil and ricotta*

69 *Cracked wheat salad with broad beans, courgettes and peas*

71 *Papardelle with broad beans, crisp ham and young spinach*

7
CEP

8
CHERRY

9
CHICORY

10
CLEMENTINE

11
COBNUT

12
FENNEL

SALLY CLARKE

It is time to own up. This book was supposed to be entitled My Favourite 25 Ingredients and was intended to be part of our restaurant's 25th anniversary celebrations in 2009.

I am not entirely sure where the time went or when the delay started or what caused it. I could blame pressure of work, lack of 'me' time, or simply the fact that I was not ready to piece my thoughts and words together, but perhaps (and I hope), it was all for the best.

At first glance this recipe book may appear to be almost totally focused on vegetarian dishes. This has not been for any conscious reason, rather for the fact that most of my favourite ingredients happen to be vegetables, fruits, salads and herbs.

There are other special foods, however, that I would never wish to lose sight of, both when I am cooking at home and in the restaurant. Fresh anchovies simply filleted and served raw with a squeeze of lemon, or crab, freshly cooked and picked with a generous dollop of mayonnaise. Turbot, arguably my favourite fish, simply roasted with herbs and olive oil. Sardines, rigid from the sea, gutted, rinsed and grilled. Duck or squab pigeon, cooked with vegetables, citrus peel and herbs, or the various cured meats from around the world such as saucisson sec, bresaola, chorizo and culatello.

Some of these ingredients have in fact been woven into the following recipes, but they tend to take a secondary role, thus allowing the chapter-heading ingredient to take centre stage. However, depending on the type of meal you wish to serve, and for which type of occasion, many of the following recipes could easily be enhanced or embellished by a fish or a meat addition. This should be entirely a taste decision and should be guided by you alone.

I tend to eat very simply if I am cooking for myself or just for one other, and that means using a small number of ingredients –

a straightforward open toasted sandwich made from a slice of ciabatta for example, with a drizzle of olive oil, a spread of ripe avocado,
a squeeze of lime and a sprinkling of sea salt and pepper could be
a perfect meal to some — whereas a growing teenager may favour a
slice or two of roasted chicken breast or cold rare-roasted beef to go
alongside it.

Similarly, when choosing a shop item 'off the shelf', I look first at the side panel where the ingredients are listed. Put plainly, the fewer the ingredients on the list, the better the product. Those with seemingly endless lists tend to include colours, preservatives, E numbers and the like. I remember my friend and mentor, *Alice Waters of Chez Panisse*, telling me many years ago that an apple needs no label or 'list of ingredients' – it is what it is – pure, simple and uncomplicated. I have tried to keep the contents of this book that way.

When the idea of this book was conceived, I decided that it should show a selection of wonderful ingredients and their uses in a variety of ways. Hopefully as you turn the pages you will find many things to suit any palate, from a dish as simple as a salad, to something quick to assemble and cook, to slightly more time-consuming desserts, ice creams and sorbets, to sweet and savoury baked items and beyond.

Nothing is overly complicated here and nothing (other than perhaps the laborious process of candying peel!) should take too long. As with so much of what we cook at the restaurant, the key is in the quality and provenance of the ingredient. If you can grow it yourself, or choose it at your local farmers' market stall you are very lucky. If you have to rely on shops or supermarkets you are likely to have to work a little harder at choosing what is the best, most sustainable, and most importantly, what has not travelled too far to get to you. Once you have collected all your ingredients, then the attention to detail of your preparation is about to start – no pressure here then!

I have always said to my staff that the majority of the work that goes into the creation of our lunch and dinner menus should be the buying of ingredients and their preparation. Once the customer has made their choice the kitchen then gets its real adrenaline rush, as the orders start to stack up on the bar.

But the cooking, assembling and garnishing of a dish, whilst technically challenging (and the timing is paramount), is very often the part of the dish's creation that takes, surprisingly, the lesser amount of time.

So take your time choosing your dish, in the selection of ingredients and then the preparation. There are many recipes in this book which can be left mid-way, to rest or to cool down, or even to improve. This allows you to plan your time more easily, as you prepare your meals.

It is important also to think of yourself when planning, as you need to feel as relaxed and unpressured as is possible when you eventually get to sit down at the table. A simple menu which does not involve too many hot elements will ease the pressure, as will the serving of a cold or room temperature first course, followed by a hot main course – or vice versa. A cold or cool first course would allow the cook time to focus on the hot main course, including its accompaniments.

The planning of a menu should not only be concerned with the selection and compatibility of its ingredients, but also the planning and preparation time, including the time it takes to serve, arrange and present.

A meal will be enjoyed far more by friends and family, when the cook is looking (and feeling) calm and composed at the table, rather than frazzled, hot and bothered at the stove. Easier said than done as I know from bitter experience, but these recipes, if followed with care, should help to build confidence in the inexperienced cook, and give guidance to others who simply need a little inspiration.

When I wrote my first book 15 years ago, I thought that I had put 'all there was to say' in one book, and that it would be my last. Over the years however, I gradually came to realise that perhaps there was a little more to explain and demonstrate. Thirty years in the restaurant, shop and bakery business have certainly been an education and a life in itself. I have met so many wonderful and inspiring people through it, as customers and as friends, from all walks of life and professions.

This book is a celebration of that time and of those people and, of course, in praise of 30 wonderful ingredients.

ALL RECIPES SERVE SIX

USE GOOD QUALITY extra virgin olive oil, Maldon sea salt and freshly ground black pepper, and free-range or organic eggs for all recipes unless otherwise stated.

APRICOT

If I had to choose one favourite fruit it would be an impossible task, as every fruit, when it has ripened to its peak, plucked freshly from the tree or bush, still warm from the sun, sliced or pulled open to reveal the delicate and perfumed interior, is a favourite.

However I do sense a certain thrill when the first apricots arrive at the kitchen door from Italy or the south of France. At first they tend to be small and firm and perhaps a little tart, but as the season progresses, they become more succulent, sweeter, softer and ideal for jams, pies, compotes and of course, for just eating by themselves.

Although our selection of jams over the years has ranged from nectarine and raspberry to peach and redcurrant to strawberry and purple fig, my all time favourite has to be the apricot and kernel jam.

We crack the stones (as in the following pages) and blanch the kernels for a few seconds to release the skins then slice the 'nuts' finely. These are then stirred into the simmering jam just as it comes off the heat before bottling. A scoop of this on yoghurt or on a freshly toasted muffin for breakfast in the cooler months can do wonders for any jaded wintery taste buds.

A SALAD WITH the combination of a fruit, seasoned with sea salt, a touch of vinegar, a drop of olive oil and a variety of leaves, with perhaps some salted nuts, can be one of life's greatest pleasures – fresh, sweet, tangy, crisp and wholesome, all at the same time.

If the apricots are not up to scratch, use white or yellow peaches, purple or green figs, pears, apples, grapes – in fact whatever looks good in your garden or market stall.

APRICOT SALAD WITH MOZZARELLA AND MARCONA ALMONDS

6 ripe apricots
A selection of salad leaves eg landcress, watercress, mizuna, red mustard leaf
50 g Marcona or other good quality almonds
3 large balls fresh buffalo mozzarella

For the dressing:
2 tbsp balsamic vinegar
4 tbsp olive oil, plus a little extra for the salad leaves
Salt and pepper
A few chives cut into 1 cm lengths

Wash the apricots, wash and spin the salad leaves, roughly slice the Marcona almonds and whisk the dressing ingredients together in a small bowl.

TO SERVE

Toss the leaves with the almonds and a little olive oil, salt and pepper. Scatter them over a platter, arranging the different colours and shapes attractively. Pull the apricots apart at their natural line (save the stones for another recipe), then cut into wedges. Tuck them in and around the leaves. Next slice or rip the mozzarella and place on top. Drizzle with the dressing, scatter with chives and serve immediately with crusty bread, or if a more robust meal is required, with slices of ham, cold chicken or cured meats such as San Daniele ham and finocchiona.

ALMOND AND APRICOT KERNEL ICE CREAM

100 g blanched almonds
6 apricot stones, or 100 g extra blanched
    almonds
750 ml milk
250 ml double cream

200 g caster sugar
12 egg yolks
50 g honey
Drop of almond essence (optional)

Roast the almonds in a medium oven (170°c) for a few minutes until pale golden, cool and chop roughly.

Crack the apricot stones with a hammer, discard the shell, remove the kernel and chop finely. Place in a pan with the chopped toasted almonds, milk, cream and half the sugar. Slowly bring to a simmer and cook very gently for 2 minutes. Cover and leave on one side to infuse for 30–40 minutes.

Whisk the egg yolks with the remaining sugar and the honey until pale, pour in the milk mixture and continue to stir until well amalgamated. Pour back into the pan and cook over a gentle to medium heat, stirring continuously, until the custard coats the back of the spoon. If it overheats, the custard will curdle so great care should be taken at this stage. Immediately remove from the heat and strain into a bowl, placed over a larger bowl of iced water. This cools the custard immediately, preventing over-cooking or curdling. Press the almond debris in the sieve with the back of a ladle to ensure the maximum amount of flavour is extracted, and keep the debris to one side. Add a drop or two of almond essence if needed.

Churn the mixture in an ice cream machine, according to the manufacturer's instructions and remove the ice cream into a freezer container, just as it becomes firm. If a chunky ice cream is preferred, stir in the almond debris at this stage. Cover and freeze for up to 12 hours before serving. It will keep well for up to two months in a freezer, but is of course best eaten as soon as possible.

APRICOTS CANNOT BE 'half baked' – the cut surfaces discolour easily and turn a rather nasty brownish-grey if the heat has not fully penetrated the fruit, so a soft, slightly melted look is what should be aimed for.

APRICOTS BAKED WITH VANILLA, CINNAMON AND LAVENDER

650 g apricots
1 vanilla pod cut in 2 lengthwise
150 ml white wine
100 g caster sugar

150 ml water
½ cinnamon stick, lightly broken
10–12 lavender sprigs (keep 6 of the
    best for decoration)

Wash and remove stems of the apricots and pull apart at the natural line. Place snugly in a terracotta or ovenproof dish (ideally the one you will serve them in) skin sides down. The fruits should be slightly overlapping at this stage as they will shrink a little on baking.

PREHEAT THE OVEN TO 180°C
In a small pan bring the remaining ingredients (except the lavender decoration) to a rolling boil for a few minutes. Pour the entire contents of the pan over the apricots and cover with aluminium foil.

Bake for 20–30 minutes, then remove the foil and continue to bake for a further 5–10 minutes or until the apricots are soft and the syrup has become deliciously fragrant. Remove the lavender and cinnamon shards for ease of serving. Arrange the fresh lavender sprigs as decoration and serve with Almond and Apricot Kernel Ice Cream (page 25).

I ONCE DISCOVERED some delicious sweet almond biscuits in a butcher's shop of all places in the Luberon, a few miles from Avignon. This shop sold not only raw meats of all descriptions, but also dishes prepared by the family, eggs, well-sourced pastas, bottled relishes and condiments. They always had a few packets of these more-ish wafer biscuits on display, tucked in a corner by the door, and I bought them every time I went there to choose my ingredients for the day. On my return to London I made enquiries as to how they were made. In the end it was, one of my French pastry chefs who came up with the answer. Croquant d'amande: crisp, sweet but with a touch of the almond's bitterness, light both to the touch and to the taste – and as it turned out, very simple to make.

CROQUANT D'AMANDE

125 g unblanched almonds
10 g apricot kernels, (page 25) blanched
   briefly in boiling water, then peeled
   (if not available use another 10 g
   unblanched almonds)

230 g caster sugar
50 g flour
Pinch salt
2 egg whites
Rice paper or silicone wax paper

Chop the almonds roughly and the kernels finely, and mix together with the sugar, flour and salt.

PREHEAT THE OVEN TO 160°C
Whisk the egg whites until very frothy, but not stiff, and fold into the dry ingredients. Line a baking sheet with the rice paper or silicone wax paper. Divide the mixture evenly into 20 teaspoons, leaving enough space between the mounds as they will spread on cooking.

Bake for 10 minutes, turn the tray around to ensure they cook evenly and bake for a further 10 minutes or until the cookies are golden and browning at the edges. Remove from the oven and cool, before carefully tearing the rice paper away from the edges of each cookie, or slide off from the silicone paper with a palette knife.

When cool serve with Almond and Apricot Ice Cream (page 25) and Apricots baked with Vanilla, Cinnamon and Lavender (page 27) or store in an airtight container for up to 5 days.

ASPARAGUS

There are a few British and Irish ingredients that, quite rightly, stand above and beyond any grown or reared by other nations — and some of these are in this book — green asparagus, broad beans, cobnuts and raspberries to name a few. And some not listed in the book — gulls' eggs, rhubarb, gooseberries, salmon and grouse for example.

Asparagus is now grown all over the world and airfreighted to any country willing to pay for it, and too many do. No other ingredient saddens me more than asparagus, when I see it on a menu out of season. Of all the asparagus I have tasted on my travels, I can honestly say that those spears from Cambridgeshire or Suffolk or Lincolnshire are the very best. From the very thin spears on sale at the beginning of the season, which need no peeling, hardly any trimming and certainly barely any cooking, to the more robust spears available at the peak of their relatively short growing time, there are types to suit every dish and every meal.

Pair a platter of swiftly cooked asparagus spears with a bowl of freshly made lemon and chive mayonnaise and a pile of poached gulls' eggs, and you have the perfect late spring meal.

ASPARAGUS FRITTERS WITH LEMON SLICES AND CHIVE MAYONNAISE

For the mayonnaise:
2 egg yolks
250 ml light olive oil
Salt and pepper
Juice of 1 small lemon
½ bunch of finely chopped chives

100 g flour
Pinch salt
125 ml sparkling water
500 g very fine asparagus
Vegetable oil
1 egg white
6 slices of lemon
A few salad leaves eg rocket or
    watercress

TO MAKE THE MAYONNAISE

In a small bowl beat the yolks together until smooth. Gradually add the olive oil, drop by drop while continually beating, until the mixture has emulsified. If it curdles, try beating an ice cube into the mix; if this fails, start with a clean bowl, a fresh egg yolk and beat the curdled mixture in little by little as before. Add the lemon juice, salt and pepper to taste. Leave covered in a cool place until ready to serve. Fold in the chopped chives just before serving.

NB *This recipe will act as the perfect base of many a mayonnaise. Instead of chives, simply add chopped basil, Dijon mustard, finely chopped red chilli, or chopped toasted almonds for a flavoured mayonnaise to suit a variety of dishes.*

TO PREPARE THE ASPARAGUS

Prepare the asparagus, trimming the coarse ends. Rinse in cold water to remove any grit and drain well. If the asparagus are not fine, cut lengthwise in half very carefully with a small sharp knife. Lay the asparagus on a clean kitchen towel and roll them up gently like a Swiss roll to dry them as thoroughly as possible. They may be left in the fridge for up to 24 hours.

Sieve the flour and salt into a bowl and gradually add the water stirring or whisking continuously until a smooth batter is formed.

PREHEAT THE OVEN TO 160°C

One-third fill a wide heavy-based pan with vegetable oil and heat to approximately 180°C. To test the heat without a thermometer, simply place a small drop of the batter into the oil. It will sizzle and turn brown within a few seconds when ready.

Meanwhile whisk the egg white in a large bowl and fold into the batter until smooth. Place the asparagus into a large bowl and pour three quarters of the batter over and around. Toss together as a salad, coating them all in a thin layer of batter. Immediately lift a few hand-fuls of the asparagus one by one into the hot oil. DO NOT overfill the pan as it will become dangerous and the temperature will drop dramatically. Remove the fritters with a slotted spoon or tongs, as soon as they are crisp and golden. Place on an ovenproof dish lined with 3 or 4 layers of kitchen paper and keep warm in the oven. Continue frying the fritters once the oil has regained its temperature each time and keep warm as before. Lastly toss the lemon slices with the remaining batter and fry in the same way until golden.

Sprinkle the fritters with salt and arrange on a warm serving dish, scatter with the lemon slices and serve with a few rocket or watercress leaves and the pot of chive mayonnaise on the side.

I HAVE OFTEN proudly admitted that my visits to Berkeley, California are only ever planned around a sequence of meals: lunch, dinner, lunch, dinner, lunch at Chez Panisse, interspersed with visits to Alice Water's Edible Schoolyard Project and the Ferry Plaza farmers' market in San Francisco.

Until two years ago, one of my favourite treats whilst staying with Alice in the Bay Area was breakfast with her at the now sadly late-departed Café Fanny, named after her daughter, which she founded in 1984, the year I opened Clarke's. It offered a light and delicious little menu throughout the day. I would order a dish of Angelo's Eggs – poached eggs formed in little dishes the shape of flying saucers, placed on crusty sourdough toast, anointed with red wine vinegar and sprinkled with dried oregano leaves. It was a great way to start the day! Happily its successor, Café Bartavelle, serves delicious food and fabulous coffee and has now become my new favourite spot in the mornings.

If you are a fan of white asparagus as I am, try the following recipe – which combines the elements of Angelo's special egg dish with one of the most sought-after ingredients in the world, white asparagus from France, Germany or Belgium – either for a lunch, a comforting supper or a special breakfast.

WHITE ASPARAGUS WITH POACHED EGG, RED WINE VINEGAR AND SOURDOUGH TOAST

18 medium white asparagus spears
Salt and pepper
25 g melted unsalted butter
2 tbsp distilled white wine or malt
  vinegar

6 large eggs
3 tbsp red wine vinegar
1 tsp fresh or dried oregano leaves
6 slices of sourdough bread

Peel the asparagus, slice away the tough end and discard. Bring a pan of salted water to the boil and cook them for up to 5 minutes in the gently simmering water until a small knife pierces them easily (they must not remain al dente). Remove carefully with tongs or a slotted spoon and with a small sharp knife, cut each one carefully in two lengthwise. Lay on a plate cut side up, tips together like soldiers and sprinkle with salt and the melted butter. Cover with clingwrap to keep warm.

TO SERVE

Bring a pan of salted water to the boil with the distilled vinegar and drop the eggs in one by one to poach for 2–3 minutes. Very carefully remove them with a slotted spoon and drain on a kitchen cloth.

Toast the sourdough bread. Divide the asparagus and butter on to to six warm plates. Place one egg on top of each, season with salt and freshly ground pepper, drizzle with the red wine vinegar and the oregano and serve immediately with toast.

ASPARAGUS RISOTTO WITH SPELT, GOAT CHEESE AND PROSECCO

1 medium leek, washed well

2 bunches asparagus
  (approximately 500 g), washed well

700 ml vegetable or chicken stock

125 g butter

3 tbsp olive oil

1 small onion, finely diced

3 bay leaves

350 g spelt or arborio rice

250 ml Prosecco or dry white wine

250 g soft fresh goat cheese

2 tbsp chopped chervil

A few chervil sprigs

Slice the leek very finely across and check for any remaining grit. Slice the asparagus on the angle finely, leaving the top tips intact. In a small pan of boiling salted water blanch these tips briefly for 20 seconds, remove with a slotted spoon and cool down on a plate and if large, cut in half lengthwise. Reserve for later.

Warm the stock to a simmer. In a heavy-based pan heat half the butter and all the olive oil until barely sizzling and add the onion and bay leaves. Stir over a medium heat until the onion becomes opaque but not coloured. Add the spelt (or rice) and stir well so that each grain is coated in the infused oil and season with salt and pepper. When the grains start to stick to the base of the pan add the Prosecco, which will be absorbed almost immediately. Then start adding the hot stock, a cupful at a time. Once half the stock is added stir in the leek and sliced asparagus, making sure that they are well blended with the other ingredients. Keep adding the stock little by little until the spelt is al dente – approximately 15 minutes (the arborio rice may need a little more liquid than the spelt).

(If you wish to save the finishing of the risotto until later, remove from the heat, spread out over a tray to cool down rapidly, cover when cold and leave in a refrigerator for up to 24 hours.)

Continue to cook over a medium heat, adding the remaining stock until the risotto has reached a creamy consistency and the spelt retains a slight 'bite'. Stir in the crumbled goat cheese, the remaining butter, the reserved asparagus tips and the chopped chervil. Cover, and allow to sit for 2–3 minutes. Pour into a warm serving dish and serve scattered with the chervil sprigs.

AUBERGINE

To me the aubergine is as close to the animal family as a vegetable can possibly be. It is meaty, dense, tender, juicy and fragrant. It may be baked, grilled, fried or roasted, partnered with garlic, lemon, herbs, tomatoes or olive oil and each time the flesh holds its shape and character. For a meat eater trying to become vegetarian, I would suggest getting to know the aubergine in its many guises.

My favourite aubergine is the pale mauve, white and purple one which looks as if someone has put a delicate paint brush to its skin. Eggplant is the American name for aubergine, and why? Because the original aubergine was white — so white it resembled a perfectly smooth-skinned egg. In fact some eggplant are still almost completely white, but I find their skin tougher and not so yielding to cook.

If the beautiful, plump, pale aubergine are unavailable, try the normal aubergine from Italy or France which are more regular in shape and deep purple all over.

Choose them ideally early in the season, before the seeds become too noticeable.

BABA GANOUSH – SMOKED AUBERGINE WITH HOME-MADE PITTA BREAD

For the baba ganoush:

3 large pale-skinned aubergines (approximately 800 g) – if pale are unavailable use normal purple aubergines

3 cloves garlic, crushed

Juice of 2 large lemons

½ tsp salt

1 tsp paprika

2 tbsp tahini

4 tbsp olive oil

2 tbsp chopped parsley

1 tbsp chopped mint

For the pitta bread:

10 g fresh yeast (or 5 g dry or 2.5 g easy-blend)

150 ml warm water

1 ½ tbsp olive oil

325 g strong white flour

Pinch sugar

5 g salt

Pinch cumin seeds

Cornmeal or polenta for sprinkling on the baking sheet

A selection of olives, lemon wedges and small mint sprigs

TO MAKE THE BABA GANOUSH

If you have access to a wood-burning fire place a grill over the embers (not the flames) and gently cook the aubergines whole, turning from time to time, until the skin is charred and the centre is beginning to soften. Wrap the aubergines in aluminium foil to allow them to continue cooking as they cool down.

Alternatively cut the aubergines in half. With a small sharp knife make a few criss cross marks on the flesh without cutting through to the skin, rub with a little olive oil, sprinkle with salt and pepper and bake in a hot oven (200°c), cut sides up, until the skin is blistered, the flesh golden and very soft at the core, approximately 45–50 minutes. If they start to burn before being completely cooked, cover with aluminium foil. Remove from the oven and wrap as before to steam cool.

Scrape all the flesh from the skin and place into a bowl with the crushed garlic, lemon juice, salt, paprika and tahini. With a hand held blender, or in a food processor if a smoother result is preferred, mix until semi-smooth, then slowly whisk in the olive oil until light and to your liking. Fold in the parsley and mint, taste and adjust the seasoning, and leave in a cool place for up to 48 hours before serving with the warm pitta bread, olives, lemon wedges and mint sprigs.

TO MAKE THE PITTA BREAD

If using fresh yeast, mix into half the water until smooth and leave in a warm place to prove. When it starts to gently foam add the remaining water and olive oil. If using the dry or easy-blend yeast, simply mix the water and oil together. Either by hand or in a mixing machine with a dough attachment, mix the liquid with the flour (and dry or easy-blend yeast if using), sugar, salt and cumin seeds and knead until smooth and shiny.

Cover and allow to prove for up to 2 hours in a warm place or until double its size.

PREHEAT THE OVEN TO 220°C

Sprinkle a little cornmeal or polenta on a baking sheet.

Remove the dough from the bowl and knead gently for a few seconds. Divide equally into 6 or 8 and shape into balls. Using a dusting of flour roll out into oval 'slipper' shapes and lay each one on the prepared baking sheet.

Just before placing them in the oven, flip them over one by one so that the cornmeal coated side is uppermost. Bake for 8–10 minutes or until puffed and golden brown.

Eat as soon as possible with baba ganoush, hummus, taramasalata or Greek salad.

BAKED AUBERGINE, COURGETTE AND TOMATO WITH RICOTTA

2 aubergines, approximately 600 g
Fine salt
500 g large ripe plum tomatoes
2 cloves garlic, finely chopped
3 tbsp olive oil
2 tsp chopped marjoram
Salt and pepper
2 courgettes

Light olive oil for frying
2 tsp chopped thyme
250 g ricotta
40 g butter
40 g plain flour
400 ml milk
2 bay leaves
60 g Parmesan, grated

Wash the aubergines and cut into ½ cm slices, place in a colander, sprinkle generously with the fine salt and leave to drain for up to an hour.

Blanch the tomatoes in boiling water for 5–10 seconds or until the skin easily peels away. Remove from the water and quickly place in a bowl of iced water to chill them and arrest the cooking. Peel, quarter and de-seed the tomatoes, retaining the debris for another use. Cut the tomato pieces into halves, place in a bowl with the garlic, olive oil, chopped marjoram and pepper and toss gently.

Cut the courgettes into ½ cm slices and fry in a heavy-based frying pan with enough olive oil to cover the base, until just beginning to colour and soften. Remove with a slotted spoon and leave on one side.

Rinse, drain and pat dry the aubergine and fry in the same pan with a little extra olive oil until the edges start to colour. This is best done in small batches.

PREHEAT THE OVEN TO 175°C
Choose a flat ovenproof dish which will easily contain all the vegetables. Layer the aubergine and courgette overlapping together, season with salt and pepper and half the chopped thyme and then scatter over the tomatoes. Crumble the ricotta into pieces the size of walnuts, placing them evenly over the top.

Heat the butter in a small pan, add the flour and cook for a few minutes over a medium heat without colouring. Add the milk little by little with salt and pepper and bay leaves. Cook gently until it has thickened. Off the heat add almost all the grated Parmesan. Remove the bay leaves from the sauce and pour over the surface of the vegetables, covering most but not all (it is good to see a few pieces of vegetable peeking through). Sprinkle with remaining chopped thyme and remaining Parmesan. Place the dish in the oven and bake for 30–35 minutes or until golden on the surface and piping hot throughout.

TO SERVE
Either hot as a light supper or lunch dish or cold with salad leaves, ciabatta and a delicious rosé wine.

THIS SICILIAN SWEET-SOUR aubergine dish made with pine nuts, red wine vinegar and celery has, most probably, as many versions of it in the world, as there are versions of ratatouille or salade niçoise, and I suspect there are as many arguments over the authenticity of the list of ingredients. However this recipe is the one we favour at the restaurant and shop – for its colour, texture and delicious balance of sweetness and acidity. Choose the round pale aubergine for preference.

CAPONATA

2 medium aubergines, approximately 600 g
1 tsp fine salt
1 small onion, peeled
1 stick celery, washed
½ fennel bulb, washed
A few tbsp light olive oil
2 cloves garlic, crushed to a paste
Salt and pepper
1 tbsp chopped marjoram or parsley

1 tsp chopped thyme
300 g ripe tomatoes or 300 g good quality canned chopped tomatoes
1 tbsp Demerara sugar
3 tbsp red wine vinegar
A few large capers and good quality olives, pitted
1 tbsp pine nuts toasted in a little olive oil until golden
2 tbsp roughly chopped flat-leaf parsley

Wash and remove the stalk of each aubergine and cut into cubes, approximately 1 cm. Place in a colander, sprinkle with the fine salt and leave to drain for up to 1 hour.

Dice the onion, celery and fennel and cook over a high heat in a heavy-based frying pan, with enough olive oil to cover the base, stirring continuously until the vegetables start to colour. Add the garlic, salt and pepper to taste, marjoram and thyme and stir well. Pour all these ingredients into a large pan which will eventually contain the aubergine as well.

If using fresh tomatoes bring a small pan of water to the boil, blanch them for a few seconds, remove with a slotted spoon and cool rapidly in a bowl of iced water. Peel them, then chop roughly.

Wipe the frying pan clean and add enough olive oil to cover well the base of the pan. Rinse the aubergine with cold water, drain and pat dry with a kitchen towel. Heat the olive oil until almost smoking, add

the aubergine carefully (it may spit in the hot oil), and fry, stirring occasionally, until the edges start to turn golden. Once the aubergine has taken on a chestnut brown colour, stir in the chopped tomato, sugar, red wine vinegar, capers and olives. Bring to the boil and then add them to the larger pan stirring carefully to avoid squashing all the ingredients. Place over a medium heat and bring to a simmer, stirring continuously to avoid sticking. Continue to cook for a few seconds or until the caponata has softened a little. Off the heat, add the toasted pine nuts and roughly chopped parsley and taste for seasoning. It should be sweet, vinegary, olive oily and piquant.

Although it is lovely served immediately, this dish improves on keeping, and will be tasty for up to 4 or 5 days if left tightly wrapped in the fridge.

TO SERVE
Serve on its own or as an accompaniment to grilled fish, chicken, veal or pork or with warm crusty bread, with soft cheeses or a dollop of crème fraîche.

BASIL

Could I say which is my most favourite herb? I doubt it. *As with trying to choose a favourite salad or fruit*, it really all depends on the menu, the occasion and of course where the herb has come from. Some freshly picked parsley from a friend's garden would taste, and be, more wonderful than a bunch of basil picked last week in the Middle East and flown to the London markets in a plastic bag. Basil has played a huge role in so many cultures and in so many ways for centuries. From India and Indonesia to France and Greece, it has been, and is still being, used in so many dishes. Of course we think of Italy as having championed it and perhaps for its rise in popularity over the past few decades. Pesto, of course, and many tomato sauce, pizza and pasta dishes call for basil as their vital ingredient.

Relatively easy to grow in Britain, we are lucky at the restaurant to have constant supplies of it, normally from *April* onwards, throughout the summer and autumn months.

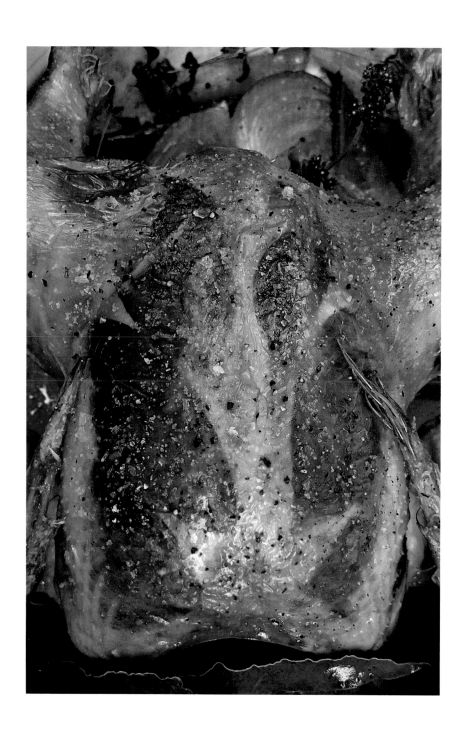

ALMOST AS CLASSIC as tarragon with chicken, basil is a perfect match – both in salads, soups or a simple roast such as this. At the restaurant in the summer we often tuck a basil leaf or two under the skin of the chicken breasts, just before roasting. The skin perfectly protects the delicate leaves, and allows the green shape to be visible when served. I love the look of the sliced chicken breast on the plate, showing the basil sandwiched between the juicy meat, and the crisp golden skin.

ROASTED CHICKEN WITH BASIL

1 x 2.5 kg organic or free range chicken
1 bunch basil
1 medium onion, peeled and roughly chopped
1 carrot, peeled and roughly chopped
2 sticks celery, washed and roughly chopped
1 small leek, cut lengthwise, washed and roughly chopped

1 small fennel bulb, washed and roughly chopped
A few bay leaves and sprigs of thyme
50 g butter
2 tbsp olive oil
2 cloves garlic crushed to a cream
Salt and pepper
500 ml light chicken stock
150 ml white wine

A beautiful organic chicken may take a little longer to cook than a lesser fowl, but the flavour will be well worth the wait.

Trim the excess fat and skin from the neck end and remove the parson's nose. Pick the leaves from the basil and roughly chop the stalks. Keep a few of the small basil sprigs or leaves for garnish.

Using your fingers (nails cut short and no bejewelled fingers ideally!), gently lift the neck end skin away from the breast meat as far as possible towards the leg end and over the thighs. Place as many large basil leaves as you can in one layer over the meat, then press the skin back down firmly into the original shape.

PREHEAT THE OVEN TO 180°C
Place the vegetables, bay leaves, thyme and basil stalks in a heavy oven dish or roasting pan and then the chicken, breast side up. In a small pan heat the butter and olive oil with the garlic and pour this evenly all over the chicken. Season with salt and pepper.

Roast for 20 minutes or until the skin has started to colour. Turn the oven down to 170°C and continue to cook for 30 minutes.

Remove from the oven and with tongs carefully turn the chicken over. Pour the stock into the roasting pan and return to the oven for a further 40–50 minutes or until the juices of the thigh run clear when pierced with a skewer. Remove the chicken to a bowl and cover either with a lid or clingwrap.

Meanwhile skim the excess fat from the roasting dish and scrape the vegetables and juices into a small pan. Bring to the boil with the white wine, remaining basil leaves and any juices which may have drained from the chicken. Simmer for a few minutes, skimming if necessary, then strain, taste and adjust the seasoning. Serve the chicken whole, garnished with the basil sprigs, with the sauce on the side and a dish of steamed leaf broccoli, spring cabbage or wilted spinach.

Alternatively, place the chicken on a chopping board, remove the legs and cut in two at the drumstick/thigh joint. Trim away the drumstick end to neaten. Remove the wing tips, then the two breasts whole from the breast bone. Cut these in half at a slight angle then remove the wishbone from the carcass in one piece. Place the jointed chicken on a warm serving platter and spoon the sauce over, scatter the basil garnish over and serve as above.

The carcass, trimmings (not the raw fat/skin) and vegetable debris will make a delicious stock or broth. Simply place all into a heavy-based pan, cover with cold water, add sprigs of herbs and simmer for up to an hour, skimming when necessary.

Strain, chill as quickly as possible and store in a fridge for up to three days. Remove the thin layer of fat which will have set on the surface before using. This lovely broth may be used in risottos, soups (see Chicken and Sweetcorn Soup page 270), stews or just by itself – as a pick-me-up or to ward off the 'flu'.

PALE AUBERGINE BAKED WITH
BASIL, GOAT CURD AND LEMON

2 large pale aubergines, washed
Olive oil to drizzle
Salt and pepper
1 small bunch basil, leaves removed

300 g goat curd, or fresh goat cheese
    whipped with a little double cream
Grated zest of 1 lemon, plus 1 lemon
    cut into 6 wedges for garnish
2 tsp chopped thyme

Remove the stalk end of the aubergines and cut into approximately 12 medium-fine slices.

PREHEAT EITHER A CHAR GRILL OR THE OVEN TO 180°C
Lay the slices next to each other on a work surface and drizzle with olive oil. To grill, sprinkle with salt and pepper and grill on the oiled side first, then turn over and grill again until cooked through and the bar marks are evident. Alternatively place on a baking sheet, lined with silicone wax paper, season as before and bake for 20 minutes or until golden.

Meanwhile, chop half of the basil and mix into the goat curd.

When the aubergines are cool enough to handle, lay them on the work surface as before, placing the most attractive side down. Place one or two basil leaves on top of each, then a generous scoop of goat curd, season with salt and pepper and grate the lemon zest over finely.

Roll the slices gently but firmly and skewer with a toothpick to secure. Place in an ovenproof dish, preferably terracotta, drizzle with a little olive oil and sprinkle with thyme.

Bake in the oven at 180°C for 5–10 minutes, remove the skewers and serve with lemon wedges and Tomato Sauce with Basil and Chilli (page 277) if desired.

BASIL ICE CREAM WITH SUGARED BASIL LEAVES, LEMON AND BLACK PEPPER WAFERS

For the sugared basil leaves:
1 egg white
A few small basil leaves
2 tbsp caster sugar

For the wafers:
1 egg white
50 g caster sugar
25 g flour
Zest of 1 small lemon, grated finely
25 g melted butter, cooled
¼ tsp freshly cracked black pepper

For the ice cream:
1 small bunch basil
250 ml milk
1 vanilla pod
Juice and peel of 1 small lemon
(pith removed)
4 egg yolks
80 g caster sugar
250 ml cream

TO MAKE THE SUGARED BASIL LEAVES

Whisk the egg white with a fork until very fluffy and dip the small basil leaves in one by one. Wipe the excess egg white away on the side of the bowl then place the leaves onto a plate covered in a fine layer of caster sugar. Continue until all the leaves are coated, then sprinkle them with another layer of sugar. Allow to dry, ideally overnight, in a cool place.

TO MAKE THE WAFERS

Whisk the egg white until frothy and beat in the sugar. Add the flour, lemon zest and cooled butter and mix until smooth.

PREHEAT THE OVEN TO 175°C

Line two baking sheets with parchment paper and using a teaspoon, spread 12–16 small amounts of the mixture in the shape of discs, spaced well apart as they will spread on cooking. Sprinkle each wafer with a little black pepper and bake for 6–8 minutes or until golden. Remove from the paper, cool and store in an airtight container.

If you are feeling clever however, these wafers may be moulded over a rolling pin, whilst still warm. As they cool they will form the shape of a roof tile, and you could then serve them as rather fancy French 'tuiles'!

TO MAKE THE ICE CREAM

Reserve a few large basil leaves and place the remaining bunch into the milk with the split vanilla pod and lemon peelings. Bring to the boil then remove from the heat and cover.

While the flavours are infusing, whisk the egg yolks and sugar in a bowl until pale and while still whisking, pour the milk and basil over the eggs. Stir together until blended and then cook over a low heat for a few minutes until the custard thickens. It should coat the back of the spoon when ready. Strain into a bowl over a larger bowl of iced water to stop the cooking immediately. Chop or slice the large basil leaves finely and add to the custard.

Now add the cream and lemon juice and churn in an ice cream machine, following the manufacturer's instructions.

It is always best to remove the ice cream from the machine when it is still a little soft – far better than risking an over-churned ice cream.

Cover tightly and place in the freezer. It will last up to four weeks in the freezer, but, as with most things, is best eaten immediately after becoming set enough to scoop.

TO SERVE

Scoop into pretty glass or china bowls, decorate with the sugared leaves and serve the wafers separately.

BEETROOT

As many of you will know, 30 years ago Clarke's offered a set no-choice four course menu in the evening — and only those who were unable to eat part of the meal, due to dietary constraints, were offered an alternative choice of dishes. This was never a problem for us in the kitchen as, at lunch time, our menu offered a range of dishes, so there were other ingredients readily at hand. For anyone who had a fish allergy or could not eat red meat for example, we could happily and easily adjust their menu to their requirements.

It never ceased to amaze me, however, the range of excuses some customers came up with for not being able to eat the set menu as written.

Beetroot is and was one of those vegetables that divided its fans from its detractors — and I continue to wonder why! I truly do not believe that there can be many people who physically cannot eat beetroot — rather, I now realise, that it is simply an aversion to eating a food of that colour. Of course, we are all aware of the three-days-later result, that has frightened people over the centuries — and with reason! But I do try hard to place beetroot on many of our menus throughout the year, in different guises, to gently persuade customers to try it.

W E MAKE FRESH soups daily in our Production Kitchen, both for the lunch and dinner menus and also for the shop, which allows our retail customers the joy of serving a 'homemade' soup at home without spending the time and trouble as described below.

Other than the balance of flavours, texture and liquid having to be correct, I always insist on a medium-gauge sieve being used as, whilst removing the debris such as the vegetable 'strings' and herb stalks, it allows the bulk of the soup to pass through, resulting in a silky smooth puree with very little waste.

ROASTED BEETROOT SOUP WITH DILL, BRAMLEY APPLE AND SOURED CREAM

600 g medium beetroot
2 large carrots
1 medium onion
2 sticks celery
1 small fennel bulb
100 ml olive oil
3 cloves garlic
½ red chilli (optional)
Peel and juice of 1 orange
1 small bunch dill, picked into leaves
    and stalks

Salt
1 medium-sweet apple - Braeburn,
    Jonagold or similar, for the garnish
Juice of ½ lemon
1 large Bramley apple, cored and diced
Approximately 500 ml vegetable stock
    or water
A little extra orange juice or lemon juice
    (optional)
150 ml soured cream

Wash and scrub the beetroot very well, removing the leaf end and any root tendrils still remaining. If they have very rough skins, you may like to peel them. Cut roughly into pieces approximately the size of walnuts. Peel and cut the carrots and onion in the same way. Wash and roughly chop the celery and fennel.

PREHEAT THE OVEN TO 180°C
In a shallow heavy-based saucepan (which will also serve as a roasting dish), heat the olive oil, garlic, chilli if using, and orange peel for

a few minutes until fragrant. Add the chopped vegetables and cook together over a high heat until they start to colour around the edges (approximately 5–7 minutes).

Add the orange juice, dill stalks, salt and enough water to half cover the vegetables, and bring to the boil. Place in the oven, uncovered, to roast for up to 45 minutes.

Meanwhile quarter, peel and core the garnish apple and cut into very small dice. Place in a bowl with the lemon juice and salt. Pick a few dill springs for the garnish to be used later, and chop the rest, and add this to the diced apple.

Test the beetroot with a skewer and, when almost tender, remove the pan from the oven.

Taking care, as the pan will be searing hot, add the Bramley apple pieces and enough cold water or stock to just cover the vegetables. Stir well together, bring to the boil and then simmer, covered, for 15–20 minutes or until all the vegetables are soft. Allow to cool for a few minutes, then little by little, place the contents of the pan into a food processor or liquidiser and puree until smooth. Pass through a medium-gauge sieve into a clean pan. Taste and adjust consistency if necessary. We sometimes add a touch of orange or lemon juice to the finished soup if it needs a little 'kick'.

TO SERVE
Heat or chill the soup and garnish with a dollop of soured cream, dill sprigs and a little pile of the diced apple in the middle of each bowl.

Y OU WILL NOT be surprised to learn that this version is far removed from the pallid and unappetisingly presented concoction often found in tins on some supermarket shelves and that which may have featured in some past school lunch nightmares. If the beetroot leaves are fresh and still pretty, use them as well.

Creating this dish for photography was one of the most pleasing of all for me. The shapes and colours of the vegetables which we chose were vibrant and picture-perfect. Even the little tails of the root vegetables were special.

RUSSIAN SALAD – BEETROOT WITH POTATOES, TURNIPS, CARROTS AND PEAS

300 g baby potatoes

200 g small carrots

150 g young turnips

200 g small beetroot, of various colours
  if available

2 bay leaves

100 g fresh peas (podded weight)

2 tsp Dijon mustard

1 tbsp freshly grated horseradish

1 tbsp lemon juice

250 ml mayonnaise (page 32)

Salt and pepper

A few baby capers

A few spring onions, trimmed and
  washed

3 tbsp olive oil

1 tbsp red wine vinegar

A bunch of watercress, washed, spun and
  thick stalks removed

Wash the potatoes and peel the carrots and turnips. Halve or quarter the potatoes depending on their size, slice the carrots on an angle and cut the turnips into small wedges. Scrub the beetroots, remove the leaf end and any root tendrils still attached and boil in salted water until tender. Cool in the water, peel and slice into small wedges. (Keep the water if making a beetroot or tomato soup within a few days.) Keep the beetroot separate from the other vegetables until the salad is assembled, as it will stain.

Cook the potatoes in salted water with the bay leaves until almost tender, remove with a slotted spoon and leave to cool. Next cook the turnips in this water, in the same way and remove, then the carrots.

Cook the peas in fresh boiling salted water, drain and chill immediately in iced water.

Mix the mustard, freshly grated horseradish, lemon juice and mayonnaise together and season to taste. It should be packed with flavour. Take half the dressing and mix with chilled water until the consistency of single cream. Slice the spring onions finely, keeping the green separate from the white part. Mix the potato, carrot, turnip and capers into the dressing with the white of the spring onion.

Finely shred the beetroot leaves (if any) and jumble with the beetroot, olive oil, salt, pepper and red wine vinegar, and scatter on a plain white plate. Pile the potato salad over the top, scatter with the green spring onion, then the drained peas. If the salad is assembled in this order, and carefully, the effect will be both colourful and pretty. Serve with a side salad of green or red watercress leaves and offer the remaining horseradish mayonnaise separately.

CONTRARY TO MOST beetroot recipes that involve other ingredients as well, I thought that I should give one recipe that celebrates (rather than avoids) the staining effect beetroot has on other ingredients.

The aim of baking en papillote – in essence in a parcel – is to completely seal in the juices, flavours and steam which the cooking will create. It is a fun and tasty way to prepare food. This method lends itself particularly well to fish and vegetables – but I have even tried a recipe for spaghetti baked in a bag with a fresh tomato sauce and herbs – not overly successful!

Root vegetables though are ideal for this method of cooking and it is easy enough to test if they are ready, by inserting a small skewer into the side of the bag.

Allow guests to have the pleasure of opening their own papillote at the table – the steam and aromas rising from within will be a talking point as well as being mouth-watering.

Serve alongside dishes that will show the contrasts in colour beautifully such as poached chicken, baked smoked haddock with Hollandaise sauce or baked ricotta, spinach and mint – just try your best to keep them separate on the plate.

BAKED BEETROOT AND CARROTS WITH NEW SEASON GARLIC

6 small / small-medium beetroot, plus leaves	100 ml olive oil
2 medium carrots	Salt and pepper
1 fennel bulb	1 tbsp mixed chopped herbs,
1 medium red (or white) onion	eg thyme, rosemary
6 cloves garlic (new season if possible)	A few bay leaves

Scrub the beetroot well and if young they should not need peeling. Trim away the leaf end and root tendrils. Cut into wedges, approximately 1 cm at the exterior. Wash the leaves and discard any which are discoloured.

Peel and wash the carrots and slice on the angle to 1 cm. Trim the fennel and cut into even-sized wedges from the root end to the tip.

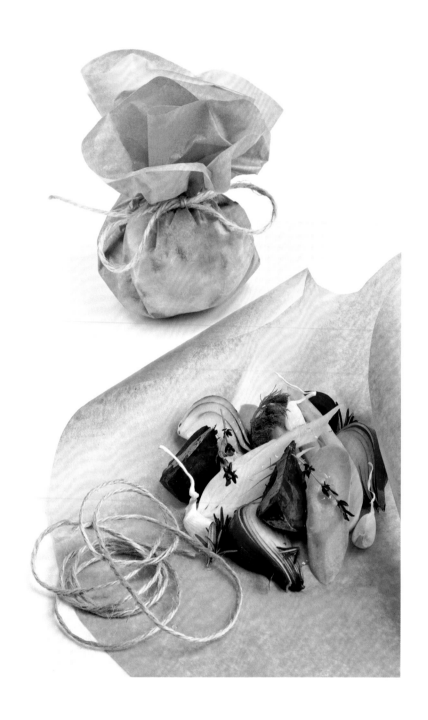

Carefully remove the root end of the onion, peel and cut into wedges as above. Peel the garlic cloves, halve and remove the green shoot, if any. Place all vegetables together into a bowl, add olive oil, salt, pepper, chopped herbs, bay leaves and the roughly chopped beetroot leaves and toss together.

PREHEAT THE OVEN TO 180°C
On a work surface place six large sheets of silicone wax paper, approximately 30 cm square. Place an even selection of vegetables into the centre of each and gather the edges up and tie with a piece of string, with a simple bow. Trim the tops of the papers if they are too tall, then place the packages into an ovenproof dish and bake for up to an hour. Test the vegetables occasionally with a skewer through the paper package – they will not resist when they are ready.

Remove from the oven and allow to cool for a few moments before placing them onto a warm serving dish. Alternatively the vegetables may be cooked in one large aluminium foil package, for up to 40 minutes, then served cold, jumbled in a bowl with a simple vinaigrette drizzled over and around and garnished with a few salad leaves perhaps.

BROAD BEAN

In every case of broad beans there will be a variety of sizes. The smallest and brightest green ones are inevitably going to yield the most tender beans which can simply be eaten raw with shavings of pecorino or with little toasts spread with ricotta. The medium- and larger-sized beans need a little more work.

I am probably more fussy about the cooking of broad beans than any other task in the restaurant kitchen during the early summer months, as it requires a great deal of attention to detail to achieve the perfect result. Even 2 or 3 seconds too long in the blanching water will change the outcome and, to my eye, the beauty of the product.

For perfection, have a pan of boiling water, the podded beans, a slotted spoon, colander and a bowl of iced water at the ready before you start. Plunge the beans into the boiling water and after a few seconds (no more than 5 for the small ones or 20 for the larger ones), remove one or two with the slotted spoon. Gently press one of the larger beans and if the skin feels 'pillowy' they are ready. Either strain through a colander or remove the beans with the slotted spoon and put immediately into the iced water. Stir them well so that they chill evenly. Strain and keep cold.

They will keep, covered in the fridge, for 2 or 3 days, but it is best to double-pod the large- and medium-sized beans as soon as possible, leaving the tiny ones whole of course, and then to eat soon after.

BROAD BEAN CROSTINI WITH LEMON, OLIVE OIL AND RICOTTA

1.5 kg unpodded broad beans
  (500 g podded)
150 g fresh ricotta
Salt and pepper
Juice and finely grated zest of 1 lemon
3 tbsp olive oil
1 tbsp chopped chives

6 slices day-old bread — baguette,
  ciabatta, sourdough
1 clove garlic
A few pea shoots or other salad leaves,
  washed
Chive blossoms if available

Grade the beans into small and large. Bring a pan of water to the boil and have a bowl of iced water at the ready – this is most important for the brightness of colour of the finished dish.

Plunge the small beans into the boiling water first and cook for 5 seconds. Remove with a slotted spoon to the iced water. Then blanch the larger beans for up to 20 seconds and ice as before. When chilled, drain and double pod the larger ones. Keep the small beans unpeeled.

PREHEAT THE GRILL

Chop the double-podded beans finely (removing any which are hard and yellow) or use a food processor.

In a mortar with pestle (or continue with a food processor) pound the beans with the ricotta, salt, pepper, and lemon zest until smooth. Gradually add the olive oil and lemon juice and a little iced water to make it a light, scoopable consistency. Fold the chives into the puree and taste.

Slice the day-old bread, place on a baking sheet, drizzle with olive oil and season with salt and pepper. Grill until golden and crisp, turn over and repeat. Rub each slice whilst hot with a cut clove of garlic, which will melt with the heat as you scrape it across the rough texture of the toasts.

Spoon the puree onto each toast, garnish with the small unpeeled broad beans, pea shoots and snipped chive blossoms and serve with an aperitif or as an accompaniment to a salad or a selection of hors d'oeuvres.

THIS SALAD COULD be made with a wide variety of grains or small types of pasta instead of cracked wheat. Spelt, pearl barley, riso nero, Puy or Umbrian lentils, fregola, orzo or bow tie pasta would all work well. Use whatever is in your cupboard.

Most recipes call for boiling water to be added to cracked wheat to make it edible, but I have never understood this. Instead I prefer to take a more flavourful approach by making a vegetable and herb broth.

CRACKED WHEAT SALAD WITH BROAD BEANS, COURGETTES AND PEAS

For the vegetable and herb broth:
1 onion, peeled and chopped
2 sticks celery, chopped
2 outside leaves fennel, chopped
1 large carrot, peeled and chopped
1 small leek, halved, washed and chopped
Bay leaves, parsley stalks, pea pods if available, sprigs of thyme or rosemary
Enough cold water to cover well the ingredients in a large pan

For the cracked wheat salad:
250 g cracked wheat
Salt and pepper
100 ml olive oil
Juice of 2 lemons
1 large or 2 small courgettes
1 tbsp finely chopped chives
1 tbsp roughly chopped parsley
1.2 kg unpodded broad beans (400 g podded weight)
200 g fresh peas (podded weight)

To serve:
Pea shoots or another salad leaf, washed

Make the vegetable broth by simmering the first set of ingredients for 20–30 minutes. Strain and measure 250 ml and pour over the cracked wheat. Any excess broth may be used for soup or risotto for example. Add salt, pepper, half the olive oil and lemon juice and stir well. While still warm, cover tightly with cling wrap and leave to soak for up to an hour.

(Alternatively cook the grain or pasta of your choice in boiling salted water, drain and rinse in cold water. Toss with a little olive oil, salt and pepper.)

PREHEAT THE CHAR GRILL OR THE OVEN TO 180°C

Meanwhile wash and trim the courgette, slice thinly (approximately ½ cm thick), lay on a plate and jumble with a little extra olive oil, salt and pepper. If using a char grill, grill on both sides until golden and bar-marked. Alternatively, place on an oiled baking sheet and roast for up to 15 minutes in the oven.

Cool before cutting on an angle, across, into short sticks. Sprinkle with chives and parsley.

Cook the broad beans as in the previous recipe, preferably using the small and the medium beans, as these will be the prettiest in the salad.

Blanch the peas in boiling salted water, strain, plunge into iced water and drain.

With a fork, fluff up the cracked wheat to separate the grains, until light and delicate.

Mix all the ingredients (including the remaining olive oil and lemon juice) together carefully but thoroughly, taste, adjust seasoning and serve with pea shoots or another summer salad leaf.

T HIS IS A perfect way to use up trimmings of the hock end of San Daniele ham, pancetta or leftover bacon.

The broad beans should either be the tiny ones (single-podded – just taken out of the pod), or the mid-sized beans double-podded (podded, then blanched, iced and peeled as described on page 67). The combination of the very bright green double-podded beans paired with the paler green single-podded ones in the same dish is very beautiful. Although the broad ribbons of papardelle suit this dish well, other types of pasta may be more readily available. If you are willing to make the pasta yourself, papardelle are among the easiest, as the ribbons are cut by hand once the rolling is done.

It is important to only briefly blanch the beans, and then immediately plunge them into iced water.

We use cream and butter sparingly in the summer, however a light amount of cream in this dish does not make it overly rich. If olive oil is preferred to cream, simply replace it, using approximately 50 ml olive oil instead.

PAPARDELLE WITH BROAD BEANS, CRISP HAM AND YOUNG SPINACH

100 g San Daniele ham or smoked
   bacon, or 200 g pancetta,
   thinly sliced and then cut into
   fine strips
1.2 kg unpodded small and medium
   broad beans (400 g podded)
500 g dried papardelle or 700 g fresh
   papardelle

200 ml cream
100 g baby spinach leaves or parsley
   leaves, washed
Salt and pepper
1 tbsp chopped mint
150 g grated Parmesan

In a frying pan, fry the ham or pancetta over a medium-high heat until crisp, turning occasionally to ensure even cooking. Drain on kitchen paper.

Blanch and ice the broad beans as described on page 67, then peel the medium ones. Mix the small and medium ones together and keep refrigerated until the dish is assembled.

To cook the pasta bring a large pan of salted water to the boil –

(adding olive oil to the cooking water is unnecessary and I dislike the habit).

Cook the papardelle (or other choice of pasta) until just cooked (it will continue cooking a little with the sauce). Strain and quickly return to the pan, retaining enough of the pasta water to cover the base of the pan. Over a high heat, add the cream (or olive oil if preferred), the spinach leaves or parsley, salt, pepper and chopped mint. Gently but thoroughly stir all the ingredients together as the spinach wilts down. Remove from the heat after a few seconds, add the broad beans and half the Parmesan, then give one final stir as it is poured into the warm serving dish. Sprinkle with the remaining Parmesan and crisp ham pieces and serve immediately.

CEP

I described in my first book the joys of foraging for mushrooms, often with my mother, in the woods in Surrey. It is an extraordinary feeling, when you suddenly realise that your eyes have at last become accustomed to the light and the colours of the flora and fauna so that, with a little luck, the mushrooms leap out and surprise you. I am fortunate to have my mother as a sounding board as I am not yet confident in the good, bad and ugly ones of the forest. Make sure you have someone you can trust to advise you too.

The cep is the king of the mushroom kingdom for me – little girolles are sweet and more-ish, chanterelles dainty and delicious, but the cep is so versatile, dense, delicate and pungent at the same time, and rare.

Never wash a cep, always brush or wipe with a damp cloth. Trim the base of the dry stalk or base if necessary with a small knife, then with a mushroom brush, remove any sand or leaf or slug.

THE OVERUSE OF the word 'carpaccio' on menus – from Glasgow to Guildford, for anything from pineapples to sea bass – has rather numbed me and, as a result, I have resisted the temptation to follow suit for almost 30 years. The delicious and famous dish of that name, served at Harry's Bar in Venice, of thinly sliced sirloin of beef with olive oil, lemon and Parmesan shavings is copied the world over, in some places with success, though not all.

This dish could join the pineapple and sea bass clan – but I prefer the title I have given it.

FINELY SLICED CEPS WITH PARMESAN, LEMON, OLIVE OIL AND PARSLEY TOASTS

250 g perfect ceps, they must be firm and without any trace of maggot infestation or discolouration

A small baguette, sourdough or country-style loaf

1 small bunch parsley

1 clove garlic

4 tbsp olive oil, plus more for drizzling

100 g Parmesan, in one piece

2 tbsp finely chopped chives

Salt and pepper

1 large lemon, cut into 6 wedges

Choose the freshest ceps you can find, then clean as described on page 75.

To make the toasts, preheat oven to 175 °C, then slice the bread very thinly. Cut each in half to make 12 little slices. Chop parsley and garlic together very finely then add to the olive oil, with salt and pepper. With a teaspoon, anoint each slice of bread with a little of the parsley paste, spreading it over the surfaces. Lay the slices, parsley side up, on a baking sheet and bake in the oven for 5–7 minutes, or until the bread is golden brown at the edges. Prepare the Parmesan, with either a potato peeler or long sharp knife, making fine shavings.

When almost ready to serve, using a small sharp knife, cut the ceps into very fine slivers and place directly onto a serving platter, one layer flat on the plate. Scatter the Parmesan over, sprinkle with sea salt and generously with chives. Drizzle with the best olive oil you can afford and serve with lemon wedges. Offer the toasts separately.

PUFF PASTRY GALETTE WITH CEPS, ROASTED ONION AND GOAT CHEESE

2 tbsp olive oil

50 g butter

1 large onion, peeled and finely sliced

1 tsp finely chopped rosemary

Salt and pepper

250 g puff pastry

250 g ceps

300 g fresh goat cheese

Heat the olive oil and butter together in a heavy-based pan and cook the onion until soft and golden, approximately 10–15 minutes. Stir in the rosemary, salt and pepper, then remove with a slotted spoon. Leave the juices in the pan.

Meanwhile roll the puff pastry into a rough square, approximately 30 cm x 30 cm and 3 mm thick, place it on a baking sheet and chill in a fridge or freezer for at least 20 minutes.

Prepare the ceps as described on page 75 and cut into quarters or eighths, depending on their size. Reheat the pan containing the onion juices and fry the ceps for a few seconds until they just start to lose their rawness. Remove with a slotted spoon and leave on one side.

PREHEAT THE OVEN TO 175°C

With a fork, prick the centre of the pastry a little, leaving a 2 cm rim around the edge – this will prevent it from puffing too much. Spread the cooled onions over the entire surface, except for the 2 cm rim. Scatter the ceps on top evenly.

Fold the edges, in an overlapping fashion, to make a crimped border to the tart, thus creating a low wall around the onions. It does not have to be perfect as this tart looks best a little rustic.

Place in the oven and bake for up to 30 minutes or until the pastry looks puffed and golden and the filling looks buttery and brown in places.

Remove from the oven and slice the goat cheese finely, and place over the top. Bake for a further 5–10 minutes or until the base is completely crisp and the cheese has started to melt a little. Slide onto a cooling rack and cool for a few minutes before serving.

OPEN CEP OMELETTE WITH THYME AND CREME FRAICHE

250 g ceps
100 g butter
2 tsp chopped thyme
Salt and pepper
1 tbsp chopped parsley

12 eggs
100 ml full cream milk
150 ml crème fraîche, room temperature
    is best

Prepare the ceps as described on page 75, trimming away any discolouration or sandy parts. Slice or wedge the ceps into even-sized pieces. In a medium-sized omelette pan heat half the butter until foaming and sauté the ceps quickly with the thyme, a little salt and pepper. Add the parsley and remove all with a slotted spoon to a small bowl, leaving the mushroom juices in the pan. Add the remaining butter to the pan and remove from the heat.

In a bowl beat the eggs with a fork, with a little salt and pepper and the milk.

Place the pan back on the heat and when the foaming butter begins to subside, pour in the eggs. With a wooden spoon gently move the cooked egg into the centre of the pan, little by little. When it is almost cooked to your liking scatter the ceps over the surface and as soon as the omelette has set, slide onto a warm plate. Serve immediately with teaspoonfuls of crème fraîche and warm crusty bread.

CHERRY

I love writing the word gâteau on the menu at the restaurant, but I feel that I do it more in jest than for any serious reason. It brings back memories of my childhood in the 60s – of the bakery shops in the High Street, their windows brimming with cakes filled with layer upon layer of (most probably) artificial creams, and of my friends who served them at birthday parties and celebrations.

In the restaurant's early days, on April 1st each year I used to plan a joke menu for our dinner customers – offering dishes such as Prawn Cocktail, Steak and Chips and Black Forest Gâteau. The prawns would have been freshly poached in a flavourful court bouillon, then peeled and marinated in a delicate lemon and lime mayonnaise and served on a bed of little spring lettuce leaves. The steak would have been cut from a piece of grass-fed Angus beef, char grilled to rare-medium-rare and garnished with a soft butter flavoured with spring herbs, cracked pepper and sea salt. The chips were, as they are now, thrice cooked – once in boiling salted water, once in fat at 160°C then finally at 190°C for the final crisping and colouring.

By the time the guests arrived at the dessert course, our famous Black Forest Gâteau, they would have got the joke and a merry time was had by all. I think that in those days I must have 'cheated' for the dessert however and used bottled cherries from France, as the fresh cherries would have been at least a month away from arriving into the UK markets.

T HIS RECIPE DEMONSTRATES how a rich dark chocolate cake, made without flour, with freshly whipped cream, cherries poached in Kirsch and a little know-how can create an exceptional version of the 1960s black chocolate sponge cake, which had, more often than not, been over-soaked in Kirsch 'flavour' (not the real thing), and then layered with over-sweet fake cream.

This is a little Black Forest Gâteau know-how…

DARK CHOCOLATE SOUFFLE CAKE WITH KIRSCH AND CHERRIES

For the cherries and the syrup:
250 g black or purple cherries, washed
75 g caster sugar
75 ml white wine or water
Juice of 2 oranges
75 ml Kirsch (or another liqueur of your choice if not available)

For the cake:
225 g dark or bitter chocolate, roughly chopped
110 g butter, plus a little for preparing the tin, with flour for dusting
4 large eggs, separated
110 g caster sugar

To finish:
75 g dark or bitter chocolate
300 ml double cream
Mint sprigs
Icing sugar for dusting

FOR THE CHERRIES

Place the cherries, including the stems, in a stainless steel pan and add the sugar, white wine or water and orange juice. Bring to the boil and then cover with a lid and simmer for up to 10–15 minutes or until they are soft and flavourful. Drain the cherries carefully through a colander and retain all the juices. Choose six perfect poached cherries with stems for decoration and keep to one side. Pit the remaining cherries, pulling them in two. Discard the stems and stones and sprinkle with half the Kirsch. Pour the syrup into a pan and rapidly boil until it has reduced by at least half. Pour this syrup over the pitted cherries and allow to cool.

Place a large bowl over a pan half-filled with just-boiled water and add the chocolate and butter. Immediately turn off the heat and allow them to melt gently over the residual steam.

Brush a loose-bottomed 20 cm cake tin with extra melted butter, place a disc of greaseproof paper on the base, brush again with butter and dust the base and sides with flour, then knock out the excess flour by banging the tin gently on the table.

Whisk the egg yolks and two thirds of the sugar until thick and light.

Stir the cooled chocolate and butter together and then into the egg mixture gently. Drain the pitted cherries and reserve the syrup.

Whisk the egg whites to soft peaks with the remaining sugar and fold into the mix. Pour half into the prepared cake tin and scatter with the pitted, drained cherries. Cover with the remaining mixture and bake in the centre of the oven for 35–40 minutes or until puffed but firm around the edges. It should remain slightly soft in the centre. Remove from the oven and cool before removing gently from the tin.

The cake will sink slightly in the centre, but this is as it should be.

TO FINISH

With a vegetable peeler shave the chocolate into curls or shards and leave in a cool place.

Whip the cream with the remaining Kirsch and a touch of the reserved syrup until stiff. Using a teaspoon scoop half the cream into six dollops onto the rim of the cake (if you are clever with a piping bag this can work also). Onto each dollop of cream, place a reserved whole cherry with the stem sticking upwards.

Next scatter the entire surface with the chocolate shavings and decorate with mint sprigs or cherry leaves if you have them and dust lightly with icing sugar.

Stir the remaining syrup into the remaining cream, until it reaches a pouring consistency and serve this as a sauce accompanying the gâteau, which should ideally be served within a few hours.

THIS RECIPE MAKES the most appealingly pretty and unusual Christmas present. Choose three 300 ml attractive jam jars, wash them meticulously and dry upside down in a warm oven as described below. These instructions will ensure a bacteria-free environment for the pickle to mature over the following months, as the jars sit on darkened shelves waiting to be wrapped and ribboned for Christmas – or eaten straight from the jar!

PICKLED CHERRIES WITH CINNAMON AND ALLSPICE

700 g black or purple cherries
450 ml red wine
250 g sugar
450 ml white wine vinegar
½ cinnamon stick
4 allspice, crushed

1 tsp white peppercorns
6 cloves
6 bay leaves
Peelings of 2 oranges – peeled with
    potato peeler

Wash the cherries twice and discard any which are very soft or discoloured.

Bring the remaining ingredients, except the orange peel, to the boil in a stainless steel pan and simmer for up to 30 minutes. It will make the kitchen smell divine – and if you are in the midst of selling your house, this is the day to invite prospective buyers to view!

Add the cherries and orange peelings to the liquid and simmer for a further 15 minutes. Preheat the oven to 130°C. Place the washed jars on a baking sheet and warm them in the oven for 3–5 minutes. Bring the lids, the pincer-end of a pair of tongs and the blade of a small knife to the boil in a pan of water. Remove the jars carefully with oven gloves and place next to each other on a clean work bench. Using the sterilised tongs remove the hot cherries carefully and divide between the jars evenly. They should come almost to the neck of the jar. Then remove the cinnamon stick, orange peel and bay leaves and place them into the jars, distributing them evenly.

Pour the hot liquid evenly into the jars, dividing the peppercorns, cloves and allspice as you go. The liquid should also reach the neck of the jar. Using the small knife, push the aromatics down, in and around

the cherries attractively. If the levels are too low, make one jar less, redistributing the cherries and juices. They will not only look better, but they will keep better if the levels of the liquid are high.

Lift the lids out of the water one by one with the tongs and, with a clean tea towel, screw them on tight. Leave them on one side until cold. Wash the jars with hot soapy water, polish dry and then store in a dark cool cupboard for up to 3 months to mature. Serve with cold meats or mature cheeses.

As much as I love an ingredient to look as close as is possible to its natural state when served, cherries occasionally need to be presented without their stones – it would be an unpleasant shock to come across a stone in a soft, warm, pillowy dessert such as this. These cherries need to be cooked, then pitted and left to soak in the spiced syrup.

WARM BUTTERMILK PANCAKES WITH POACHED BLACK CHERRIES AND CREAM

For the batter:
1 egg, separated
100 ml milk
100 ml buttermilk
150 g plain flour
1 tsp baking powder
Pinch salt
35 g caster sugar
30 g butter, melted

For the cherries:
450 g ripe cherries
100 g sugar

Juice of 2 oranges
½ cinnamon stick
100 ml water
150 ml dry or sweet white wine

To finish:
250 ml double cream
½ tsp cinnamon mixed with 1 tbsp
   Demerara sugar
Icing sugar, for dusting

To fry the pancakes:
50 g melted butter

TO MAKE THE BATTER
Make the batter by whisking the egg yolk, milk and buttermilk together. In a large bowl, sieve the flour, baking powder and salt together and stir in the sugar. Make a hole in the centre and pour the liquid into it slowly, stirring with a whisk and gradually incorporating the dry ingredients. Add the melted butter and leave on one side.

FOR THE CHERRIES
Wash the cherries and discard discoloured or bruised ones along with the stalks. Place in a stainless steel pan with sugar, orange juice, cinnamon stick, water and wine. Bring to the boil, cover and simmer for

10–15 minutes or until the cherries are completely soft. Leave to cool in the juice, then remove the stones. Leave the pitted cherries to soak in the juice.

Whip the cream to soft peaks and fold in the cinnamon and brown sugar so that it has a slight marbled effect.

PREHEAT THE OVEN TO 100°C

Whisk the egg white to a stiff peak and gently fold into the batter until completely blended.

Heat the butter in a heavy-based flat frying pan, until foaming, over a medium to high heat. Using a ladle or large spoon, pour in the batter, creating three or four pancakes at a time – making a total of 12. Once they have become golden on the base and sides, flip them over carefully with a palette knife, and cook on the other side until golden – approximately three minutes in total. Remove from the pan to a plate in the oven while the remaining pancakes are cooked. If more butter is needed heat it as before, until foaming, before adding more batter to the pan.

Meanwhile warm the cherries and syrup in a small pan and warm six serving plates in the oven.

TO SERVE

Place two pancakes on each plate, slightly overlapping, divide the cherries and syrup equally amongst them, and finish with a generous dollop of cinnamon cream. Serve immediately, dusted with icing sugar.

CHICORY

Sometimes called endive, Belgian endive or witloof (white leaf), this vegetable has, to some, an acquired taste — but I love it raw in salads or baked, roasted or braised. There are many attractive and delicious varieties, usually sent to the UK from Italian markets. Radicchio, treviso and tardivo are now commonly found on restaurant menus, but the slightly more unusual puntarelle is our salad of choice in winter or early spring.

I have even cooked Belgian endive as a soupy-stewy side dish to grilled beef — sliced on an angle into wide ribbons, with a little finely diced red onion or shallot, then slowly cooked in butter with chopped rosemary or thyme, salt and pepper.

CHICORY SALAD WITH APPLE, WALNUTS AND BLUE CHEESE

60 g walnuts (preferably fresh), roughly chopped
Olive oil
Salt and pepper
2 red and 2 white chicory, washed
A handful of parsley leaves, stalks removed

75 – 100 g blue cheese, eg Cashel Blue, Harbourne Blue or Stichelton, crumbled
150 ml soured cream
1 large or 2 small red-skinned apples, eg Braeburn, Spartan, Jonagold
A drizzle of walnut oil
1 tbsp chives, cut in 1 cm lengths

PREHEAT THE OVEN TO 170°C

Place the chopped walnuts on a baking sheet, drizzle with olive oil, sprinkle with salt and pepper and bake for 3–5 minutes or until crisp but not coloured.

Cut the bases from the chicory and separate the leaves, place in a salad bowl and scatter with parsley leaves.

In a small bowl whisk half the blue cheese until almost smooth, add the soured cream, salt and pepper and enough iced water to make it the consistency of single cream.

Just before serving, quarter and core the apple, then slice into fine slices. Toss the leaves, parsley and apple with a little walnut oil, salt and pepper until evenly coated and divide between six plates, arranging the salad decoratively and evenly.

Drizzle the dressing over and around, scatter with the remaining cheese, nuts and chives and serve.

BAKED CHICORY IN CREAM WITH GARLIC BREADCRUMBS

½ loaf of plain bread
3 tbsp chopped parsley
2 cloves garlic, crushed to a cream
Salt and pepper
6 small or 3 large white chicory,

washed
70 g butter
250 ml double cream
2 tsp chopped thyme
80 g grated Gruyère cheese

Trim most, but not all, the crusts off the bread and discard. Cut the bread into large cubes and process in a food processor to medium-fine breadcrumbs. Add the chopped parsley, half the garlic, salt and pepper and continue to process for a few seconds until pale green in colour.

Cut the chicory in quarters or eighths (depending on size) length-wise. Melt the butter in a heavy-based flat pan and heat until foaming. Add the chicory, cut side down and cook until starting to turn golden, turning occasionally, season with salt and pepper. With tongs, remove carefully to a baking dish, laying them attractively like sardines in a tin.

PREHEAT THE OVEN TO 175°C

Place the pan back on the heat and add the cream, the remaining garlic, chopped thyme, salt and pepper. Bring to the boil and reduce by a quarter, taste and pour over the chicory. Sprinkle with grated Gruyère and place in the oven for 10–15 minutes or until the chicory are almost tender when pierced with a knife.

Remove from the oven, scatter with the breadcrumbs and bake for a further 5–10 minutes or until crisp and golden.

Serve with a simple salad of green leaves or steamed spinach, cavolo nero or curly kale as a perfect lunch or supper dish. Alternatively serve the dish to accompany poached ham or baked fish such as hake, brill or haddock.

CHICORY TARTE TATIN

6 large even-sized white chicory
80 g butter
80 g granulated sugar

400 g puff pastry
1 tsp chopped thyme
Salt and pepper

Quarter the chicory and with a small knife remove the small triangular core end, without releasing the leaves.

Choose a heavy-based frying pan (approximately 24 cm across) which will also be used in the oven. Heat the butter and sugar in the pan until pale golden in colour (6–8 minutes). Remove from the heat and place the chicory in the pan with the tips of the leaves pointing to the centre. Cook over a medium to high heat, allowing the juices to evaporate, as the chicory gently cooks in the caramel. Turn the pieces with tongs occasionally to allow even cooking, but keep them constantly in the 'sun ray' configuration.

PREHEAT THE OVEN TO 180°C
Roll the puff pastry into a disc, approximately 25 mm thick and in equal diameter to the pan.

Remove the pan from the heat and place on a heat-proof mat or cloth. There should be only a little liquid remaining in the pan and it should be caramelised juices. Tip away any excess watery juices. Sprinkle with salt and pepper and the chopped thyme. Lay the pastry over the top and carefully tuck the edges in down the sides of the pan, enveloping the chicory.

Make a small incision in the centre with a knife, as a steam hole. Place on a baking sheet and bake for 30–35 minutes or until the pastry is puffed and golden. Remove from the oven and allow to cool for a few moments. Place a large serving plate upside down over the tart and with a firm hand wrapped in a thick cloth, grasp hold of the pan handle. Place the other hand, also protected by a cloth, on the base of the plate. Pressing the pan and the plate firmly and securely together, tip the pan upside down over the plate, allowing all the juices to arrive on the plate with the tarte.

This may be served either hot or warm, as a first course with a few green leaves on the side, or as an accompaniment to roasted meats such as goose, duck or pork.

CLEMENTINE

In late November or early December when the shiny clementines arrive from Spain and Italy, their leaves still attached, I know that Christmas is not far off. I love to see our shop festooned with baskets of them — and so do the customers, judging by the amount we sell. In the restaurant we squeeze them for juice, use them for an accompaniment to the cheese course, roast them in halves to garnish pigeon, duck and pork dishes, and celebrate them in sorbets, ice creams and syllabubs.

I often think that the sight of a bowl of leafy clementines is the perfect and perhaps the only necessary form of decoration on a Christmas dining table.

Probably the best thing to do with clementines however is to serve them whole at the end of a big meal — perhaps instead of dessert. Just watch your guests as they enjoy the ritual of peeling and dissecting the fruit as the conversation flows.

THE SALAD LEAVES which are available in the winter months are less varied than in the summer, but they are nevertheless vibrant in colour and usually slightly bitter to taste – which makes them a perfect partner to the clementine.

SALAD OF CLEMENTINES, FETA, PINE NUTS AND POMEGRANATE DRESSING

4 tbsp olive oil
40 g pine nuts
1 large pomegranate
8 firm clementines, 2 for juice and 6 to peel
Salt and pepper
200 g barrel-aged feta, chilled for ease of slicing

1 celery heart, leaves and sprigs picked from stalks
300 g salad leaves, eg escarole, trevise, castelfranco, red chicory, watercress, washed

In a heavy-based frying pan, heat the olive oil and pine nuts together over a medium to high heat, stirring continuously, until the nuts have turned golden evenly. Remove from the heat and allow to cool.

Cut the pomegranate across the equator and, holding each half over a bowl, remove the seeds by knocking the shell with a rolling pin. Discard the white pith, if any, and drain the juice into a small bowl. Add the clementine juice, salt, pepper, pine nuts and the olive oil. Mix well together, taste for seasoning.

Slice the feta finely with a small sharp knife – it will crumble but that is part of its charm.

Carefully peel the remaining clementines and scrape away any excess pith, then slice each into 3 or 4 across the segments.

Cut the small sprigs of celery leaves from the celery heart and slice the tender stalks finely on the angle. Place these with the salad leaves in a large bowl and toss with the dressing. Pile onto a platter, dividing the pine nuts evenly. Tuck the clementines in and around and scatter over the feta. Finally sprinkle with the pomegranate seeds and serve immediately. This lovely fresh salad is perfect for accompanying cold roasted meats or fowl or simply by itself alongside crusty garlic bread.

CCASIONALLY I TREAT myself to a cocktail – a Negroni – which is made with Campari, sweet vermouth and gin, although I usually substitute vodka as I find it interferes less with the fragrant, heady, herbal tones of the Campari.

Although I tend to be a 'wine with food' person rather than a 'going out for a drink' person, I sometimes choose a Campari with pink grapefruit juice or with sparkling water as an aperitif – it is refreshing, very pretty and thirst-quenching.

The combination of the slight bitterness of Campari with the sweet but astringent juice of the clementine, and a hint of vanilla as in this sorbet, is a magical one. It is perfect for serving after a rich main course as dessert, or as part of a selection of desserts.

As sorbet is often not easy to handle in a hurry, this can be scooped in advance and left in the freezer, either in individual glasses or in a large serving bowl, which makes the serving easier.

CAMPARI, CLEMENTINE AND VANILLA SORBET WITH CLEMENTINE ZEST MADELEINES

For the sorbet:
100 ml water
200 g caster sugar
½ vanilla pod, split lengthwise
600 ml freshly squeezed clementine
  juice (15–20 clementines)
150 ml Campari

For the madeleines:
Zest of 3 clementines
2 eggs
110 g caster sugar
110 g flour, plus extra for preparing
  the tin
90 g melted butter, plus extra for
  preparing the tin

FOR THE SORBET

Bring the water, sugar and vanilla pod to the boil and simmer for 5–10 minutes or until some of the vanilla seeds have been released. When cool, scrape a few more seeds into the syrup, rinse the pod and keep for another use.

Add the clementine juice to the syrup and then the Campari. Stir well and pour into an ice cream machine and churn following the

manufacturer's instructions. Just before it is firm, scoop into a freezer container and freeze for up to 1 week, although this sorbet will be best served within a few hours. Serve with a warm madeleine on the side.

FOR THE MADELEINES

Clementines are not as easy as oranges to zest – as they are softer and smaller – it is tricky to get any 'purchase' on the fruit whilst grating the rind. The important part is not to collect any pith as you grate, so slowly and gently does it.

Lightly whisk the eggs and sugar with the clementine zest until very frothy. Using the whisk, fold in the sieved flour and then the cooled butter. Leave to rest for up to 30 minutes, covered in a cool place.

PREHEAT THE OVEN TO 180°C

Brush the madeleine moulds generously with soft butter, sprinkle with flour and knock out the excess. This will ensure that the little cakes, once cooked, fall out of the moulds with ease.

With a dessert spoon or large teaspoon, scoop the filling into the moulds, almost to the rims. Bake for 10–12 minutes, or until they are puffed and golden. Leave to cool for a few minutes then tap them out of the tin and serve as soon as possible.

W INTER DEMANDS THAT we eat well and in quantity. We need comforting and warming and this usually means big bowls of steaming broth, or soups and sauces made with butter and cream instead of the lighter, fresher flavours that olive oil can offer us in the summer. Long, slow-braised meats and game nourish the eye as well as the soul, especially when partnered with soft polenta made rich with Parmesan and butter, or potatoes roasted in duck fat and herbs.

However, a meal cannot be filled with comfort alone. A bright, perhaps sharp or astringent note needs to be added to a winter menu, not only to 'cut' the richness, but also to enliven taste buds that have perhaps been somewhat dulled by so much carbohydrate and protein.

This very simple but beautiful salad can warm the heart just by looking at it. It will bring a new dimension to the selection of winter dishes normally served during the festive times and will not only aid digestion towards the end of a meal, but refresh the spirit too.

CHRISTMAS AND NEW YEAR'S EVE FRUIT SALAD

1 large pineapple
4 passion fruit
Juice of 3 limes
Juice of 4 clementines

2 firm but ripe mangoes
12 firm clementines (or mandarins)
Mint sprigs (if available)

Remove the good-looking leaves of the pineapple, wash and cut the base of each leaf decoratively at an angle. Leave on one side.

Cut the top and base from the pineapple and standing it firmly upright on a chopping board, slice off the skin from top to bottom with a sharp knife. Trim the 'eyes' with a potato peeler. Cut the pineapple in quarters from top to bottom through the core. Remove the core then thinly slice the quarters at an angle. Leave covered in the fridge.

Cut the passion fruit in half and scoop out the seeds and juice into a small bowl. Add the lime juice and clementine juice and whisk with a fork to break up the passion fruit pulp.

Peel the mangoes, slice off the two flat sides, then the two short sides. Cut the mango into neat dice and add to the passion fruit.

Squeeze the fibrous stone over the fruit, allowing all the remaining juices to be added.

Peel the clementines, keeping them whole, and then carefully scrape away the white pith with a small knife.

Cut the clementines through the equator and gently break the halved segments apart. Place in a glass serving bowl, scatter over the pineapple slices and then pour the passion fruit mixture over and around.

Just before serving, toss very gently together so as not to break up the fruit too much. Serve decorated with the pineapple leaves scattered around and mint sprigs if available.

Serve with a sorbet, a slice of your favourite panettone or little sweet biscuits.

COBNUT

Cobnuts arrive from Kent around late September and we dive into them with gusto. Cracked and roasted whole with sea salt and olive oil, crushed in basil pesto or sliced, baked and sprinkled on salads — all are a delight and lift the spirits.

I remember planning a menu for *Alice Waters* when she was visiting England one autumn a few years ago. I knew that she was fascinated by cobnuts and, as to my knowledge they are not found in *America*, I wanted to make sure that she had plenty of opportunities to taste them.

To start with they are so pretty — the way that they grow in little clusters, their early autumnal soft green hues on the leaves and the pale nutty brown tinge to the shells are breathtaking. No wonder *Alice* loves them so much.

My menu for her was centred around the following dishes — and each was a success!

I REMEMBER NUT cutlets being part of my O-level syllabus – a dish to appeal to vegetarians. Strangely enough the textbook stated that it was first shaped into a flat patty, then with the aid of a bent thumb, an indentation should be made on one side, before cooking. Presumably this was so that your poor vegetarian guest would not feel any embarrassment by not eating a real lamb cutlet! How far we have come since those days – when, to be a vegetarian now, is seen by many as sensible as being a non-smoker.

NUT CUTLET

200 g shelled cobnuts (or hazelnuts if not available)
A little olive oil
Salt and pepper
50 ml olive oil
15 g butter
1 medium onion, peeled and finely diced
2 cloves garlic, crushed to a cream
2 tsp finely chopped sage
100 g lentils
250 g spinach leaves, washed

1 medium parsnip, peeled
1 egg
Small handful of fresh breadcrumbs (page 94)
3 tbsp flour, seasoned with salt and pepper
1 egg, whisked with a splash of milk
Dried breadcrumbs (page 139)
Olive oil for frying
Soured cream

PREHEAT THE OVEN TO 170°C

Place the nuts on a baking tray and drizzle with olive oil, salt and pepper. Bake for 5–7 minutes or until pale golden. Cool and chop by hand or, if using a food processor, process not too finely.

In a heavy-based pan, heat the olive oil and butter, add the onion and cook until soft, but not coloured. Add the garlic and sage, season generously with salt and pepper and remove from the heat.

Cook the lentils in boiling salted water until very tender (15–20 minutes), drain and cool.

Steam the spinach leaves with a little salt, drain in a colander, squeeze by hand until almost dry and then chop roughly.

Grate the parsnip coarsely into a bowl and add all the ingredients above. Lightly whisk the egg and pour into the mixture, mixing gently. Little by little add the fresh breadcrumbs until it is soft and malleable.

Taste for seasoning and shape into 12 small balls. Leave covered in the fridge for up to two hours.

Shape into flat patties, and one by one dip into the seasoned flour, egg wash and then the dried breadcrumbs. This process is best done with a friend – one person should handle the dry ingredients and one the egg wash. If the same person struggles with both tasks, fingers and hands soon become embedded in an egg and crumb mess – wasting not only the ingredients but time too.

To cook, heat the olive oil in a shallow heavy-based pan and cook in small batches until crisp on both sides, approximately 3–5 minutes. Drain on kitchen paper and sprinkle with salt. Serve with a generous dollop of soured cream and a salad of celery heart and apple.

THIS PRETTIEST and most delicious of salads can be assembled in the late summer – the figs at their most ripe and peaches at their juiciest.

As with all fruits and vegetables in this book, it is vital to choose the ones at the peak of their ripeness. The squashed misshapen figs in a basket are usually the most luscious, and you will find those shoppers at the market stalls who know best pick them out above any other. With peaches however, a little firmness is required, so that they may be beautifully sliced into this salad, whereas the figs can simply be pulled apart. (Can you not feel the heat from the sun on the back of your neck as you think of this?!)

COBNUT SALAD WITH FIGS AND PEACHES

2 bunches watercress and 1 small escarole lettuce or another selection of salad leaves

150 g shelled cobnuts or hazelnuts, cut roughly in halves

4 tbsp olive oil, plus a little for salad leaves

2 tsp balsamic vinegar

2 tsp pomegranate molasses (optional)

Salt and pepper

A few (preferably wild) blackberries

3 large ripe figs, green or purple

3 large ripe peaches

1 tbsp finely chopped chives

Pick the salad, discarding any thick stalks or discoloured leaves and rinse in very cold water. Spin gently in a salad spinner or roll in a clean tea towel.

PREHEAT THE OVEN TO 175°C

Place the nuts on a tray and toast in the oven for a few minutes or until golden and fragrant. Allow to cool.

Mix the olive oil, balsamic vinegar, pomegranate molasses, salt and pepper and taste.

In a small pan place the blackberries and a splash of water, cover with a lid and heat gently for a few minutes or until the fruit has started to soften and 'bleed' its juices. Allow to cool and add to the dressing.

Rinse the figs and peaches gently, snip the tops off the figs and cut into quarters. Cut the peaches in half and twist apart. If the stones stick rigidly to the flesh, cut the flesh away from the stone with a sharp knife, in thick slices, each time aiming the blade towards the stone.

Toss the leaves with the roasted cobnuts, a little olive oil, salt and pepper and arrange attractively on six individual plates. Tuck the peach slices and fig pieces in and around the leaves, spoon the dressing over and scatter generously with the chives.

For a more robust dish this salad lends itself to an addition of buffalo mozzarella, soft goat cheese, shavings of pecorino or crumbled feta cheese, with baked garlic-herb toasts.

ROASTED SQUAB PIGEON SALAD WITH ORANGE, ROSEMARY AND COBNUTS

6 squab pigeons
1 tbsp chopped rosemary
Salt and pepper
A little olive oil
1 tbsp orange zest

For the pigeon stock:
1 medium onion, peeled and roughly chopped
1 medium carrot, peeled and roughly chopped
2 sticks celery, washed and roughly chopped
½ leek, washed well and roughly chopped
2 outside fennel leaves, washed and roughly chopped
50 g butter

3 cloves garlic, crushed
A few thyme or rosemary sprigs
A few peppercorns
150 ml red wine
Juice of 2 oranges
250 ml chicken stock or water

To finish:
150 g shelled cobnuts or hazelnuts
A little olive oil
1 tbsp chopped rosemary
3 medium shallots, finely chopped
2 tsp redcurrant jelly (optional)
400 g green beans
A few handfuls of baby spinach leaves, or a few other salad leaves of your choice, stalks removed, washed and spun

Remove the two halves of pigeon from the carcass by cutting along the breast bone, keeping the knife close to the bone. Continue moving the knife down towards the table, around the rib cage, on each side, until you reach the ball and socket joints of the thighs. These joints can be detached with the point of the knife and the two halves of the bird will be released from the carcass. Trim away the excess fat or skin and lay these pieces skin side down on a dish. Sprinkle with rosemary, pepper, olive oil and orange zest. Cover with cling film and place in the fridge to marinate for at least 2 hours or up to 48 hours.

TO MAKE THE STOCK
Roast the carcasses in a 175 °C oven until crisp and dark brown, though not burnt – approximately 20 minutes.

In a heavy-based pan, brown the chopped vegetables in butter, then

add the garlic, herb sprigs and peppercorns. Add the roasted bones, red wine, orange juice and chicken stock or water to barely cover. Bring to the simmer and cook very gently for 2 hours, skimming occasionally. The liquid level should not reduce too much, however if the level reduces to below the line of the carcasses, top up with a little water.

Strain through a fine-meshed sieve and leave to cool before storing in the fridge. Do not remove the small layer of fat which will settle on the surface, as this will protect it until ready for use (up to three days later).

TO FINISH THE DISH

Slice or chop the cobnuts roughly, spread out over a baking sheet, drizzle with olive oil, salt, pepper and chopped rosemary. Bake in a 175°C oven until crisp and golden, then cool on the tray.

Heat a little olive oil in a wide heavy-based pan and sear the squab pigeon halves skin side down until brown, turn them over with tongs, sprinkle with salt and cook again for up to 4 minutes or until cooked to your liking. Place on a warm plate and cover for up to 30 minutes. Meanwhile add the chopped shallots to the juices in the pan with a splash more olive oil if needed, stir over medium heat until golden, add approximately ½ litre of the pigeon stock and bring to the boil. Reduce by approximately half or until the sauce is dark and shining. Taste and adjust seasoning – add a little redcurrant jelly if it needs sweetening. Strain and keep warm.

Carefully remove the legs from the breasts of the squab pigeon and slice each breast in half, on the angle.

TO SERVE

Blanch the green beans for 1–2 minutes in boiling salted water, until al dente. Drain and toss with a little olive oil, salt and pepper and scatter on a warm serving platter. Add the toasted cobnuts to the salad leaves and toss with olive oil, salt and pepper, then scatter over the beans evenly. Place the squab pigeon pieces on top and drizzle with a little of the sauce. Serve with the remaining sauce and with warm crisp potatoes or herbed wild rice.

FENNEL

I have often thought that if I had to live on one vegetable alone it could possibly be the fennel bulb. I love its shape, texture, the aniseedy smell as a knife cuts through it — and it is so versatile too. At the restaurant we shave it wafer thin and toss it with summer salad leaves, giving height to the plate and a colour contrast to the greens, yellows and reds surrounding it.

Roasted wedges of fennel make a perfect partner to fish dishes and, if baked in half with a drizzle of olive oil and herbs, it can create a bed for any number of main course ingredients to sit on.

The leaves — the little wisps of fennel which grow from within the heart — should never be trimmed away. They are full of flavour and are valuable too. Use them chopped and sprinkled on the finished dish or roasted as part of the bulb.

S OME, IF NOT all, of the best dishes in the world are the least complicated (as I am hoping this book will demonstrate) and this is a classic example of how tempting and beautiful a few fresh ingredients can be when they are carefully assembled at the last minute, with an eye on quality and provenance.

SALMON WITH SLICED FENNEL, LEMON AND DILL

---

450 g fillet of wild or organically-reared salmon
1 medium fennel bulb, washed
1 small bunch radishes

1 small bunch dill, stems removed
Juice of 2 lemons
4 tbsp olive oil
1 lemon, cut into 6 wedges

Ask your fishmonger to pin-bone the salmon for you if you are unable to do this yourself. This is essential as you will be slicing the fish raw and cardboard (not paper) thin. Any stray hair bones will drag with the knife and the slices will rip as you cut, so it needs to be done correctly.

Freeze or chill the fish in a fridge for up to 20 minutes to make the slicing easier.

Trim the fronds from the fennel bulb and chop finely. Remove the outside leaves of the fennel and use for another recipe (soup, stock, stew).

Cut the fennel heart in half lengthwise and, with the cut surface face down, slice as finely as possible in long slices. Wash and trim the radishes and slice very finely from top to bottom.

Pick a few beautiful dill sprigs and roughly chop the rest.

Place both the fennel and radishes in a bowl with the chopped fennel tops and chopped dill and chill until ready to assemble.

With the skin of the salmon flat on the cutting board, and with a very sharp long thin-bladed knife, slice the salmon thinly, slightly at an angle towards the skin. Do not allow the knife to cut through the skin; instead, angle the knife so that it just scrapes above it as the slice is released each time. Place the slices one by one onto a flat serving platter, either spread out flat or slightly overlapping.

This may now be covered tightly with clingwrap and left in the fridge for up to 2 hours, or finished immediately (which is preferable).

Toss the fennel and radishes with the lemon juice, olive oil, salt and pepper until well coated. Do not worry if there seems to be too much dressing as this will act also as the marinade for the fish. (As the lemon juice and the acidity of the olive oil touch the fish, they will start to 'cook' it, thus tenderising it slightly.)

Scatter the vegetables over the fish lightly and evenly, then drizzle the remaining juices over and around.

Garnish with lemon wedges and reserved dill sprigs and serve with granary bread or rye toasts.

FENNEL A LA GRECQUE

3 medium fennel bulbs
1 small onion, peeled and sliced into
  wide rings
4 bay leaves
1 tbsp coriander seeds, lightly crushed

150 ml white wine
Peelings and juice of 1 lemon
150 ml olive oil
150 ml water
A few sprigs of parsley, leaves and stalks

Wash the fennel bulbs and cut in half lengthwise. Remove the outside leaf or leaves until each fennel heart is roughly the same size and depth. Trim the tops at a slight angle, then shave off the discoloured root, if any. It is important to prepare the fennel in this order as if the root is trimmed too early or too much, the bulb will fall apart during cooking.

Bring the remaining ingredients, except the parsley leaves, to the boil in a wide heavy-based pan, large enough to hold all the fennel snugly.

Place the fennel hearts in the liquid, bring back to the simmer, and cover with a piece of greaseproof paper. Press a lid or plate down on top of the paper, inside the pan, thus gently submerging the fennel in the liquid.

Simmer slowly for 40–50 minutes, checking occasionally with a skewer to test if done. The fennel should be tender through to the core. Remove from the heat and allow to cool, covered.

With a slotted spoon, remove each piece of fennel to a flat dish, cut side up. Strain the liquid over, retaining the debris. Carefully place the attractive-looking pieces of marinade over the top of the fennel, such as the lemon peel, a few coriander seeds, slices of onion and bay leaves. Scatter with parsley leaves and serve cold.

This dish improves on keeping – up to four days, covered in the fridge.

CHOOSE A BEAUTIFUL line-caught sea bass from your fish-monger and ask for it to be gutted, with scales and gills removed. If you prefer not to serve the fish whole (ie with head on) ask for this to removed at the same time. If you prefer to roast the fish in fillets (ie boned) ask for this to be done for you.

SEA BASS BAKED WITH POTATO AND FENNEL

1 whole sea bass, approximately 2.5–3 kg	Salt and pepper
3 large Désirée or other roasting potatoes	4 bay leaves
	Peelings of 1 orange
2 fennel bulbs	1 bunch dill, stalks and leaves picked separately
1 tbsp fennel seeds	
60 ml olive oil	100 ml orange juice

Rinse the fish in very cold water and dry inside and out with kitchen paper.

Wash, peel and slice the potatoes thickly. Wash and cut across the fennel in medium-fine slices, keeping the leafy fronds for later.

In a small pan toast the fennel seeds until fragrant (a few seconds), then crush in a mortar with a pestle or with the bottom of a small heavy pan on a chopping board.

In a roasting tin, or wide shallow terracotta dish, place the vegetables with the olive oil, salt, pepper, bay leaves, orange peel, half the picked dill leaves and half the crushed fennel seeds. Jumble together by hand until well amalgamated and spread out flat.

PREHEAT THE OVEN TO 170°C
Roast the vegetables for 15 minutes, remove from the oven and stir gently to prevent the pieces from sticking to the base.

Meanwhile fill the cavity of the fish with the fennel fronds, dill stalks and the remaining dill, and then season generously with salt and pepper. Place the sea bass on top of the vegetables, drizzle with the olive oil, sprinkle with the remaining fennel seeds and return to the oven for up to 45 minutes or until the fish flakes easily away from the bone. To test if it is done, insert a small knife into the fish next to the dorsal fin (top fin). If the fish is cooked it will easily pass through to the bone.

If fillets are used, roast the vegetables first for 20–25 minutes until almost tender, then lay the fillets on top, skin sides up, sprinkle with fennel seeds, fennel fronds, remaining dill leaves, salt, pepper and olive oil. Bake for a further 10–12 minutes or until the skin is crisp.

Five minutes before the end of the cooking time, remove from the oven, pour the orange juice over the vegetables (not over the fish skin), and bake until the vegetables have partially absorbed the juices and the skin of the fish is beautifully crisp.

Serve straight from the oven in the baking dish, or serve slightly cooled with garlic and orange zest mayonnaise.

GARLIC AND ORANGE ZEST MAYONNAISE

2 egg yolks
1 tsp Dijon mustard
1 clove garlic, crushed to a cream
50 ml olive oil and 50 ml corn or vegetable oil

Salt and pepper
Juice of ½ lemon
Juice and finely grated zest of 1 orange

Use the freshest farm eggs and a combination of the best quality olive oil and a lighter corn or vegetable oil. The garlic should ideally be new season, with the green shoot (if present) removed.

Place the yolks in a bowl with Dijon mustard and crushed garlic and whisk until smooth. Gradually, and very slowly add the olive oil, whisking continuously until the mixture starts to thicken. Continue to add the corn oil in the same way, followed by the salt, pepper, lemon juice, orange juice and zest. If the mixture starts to separate, add an ice cube to the mix, beating vigorously until it amalgamates again. If this fails, start with a fresh egg yolk in a fresh bowl, beating the separated mixture into it very slowly. Taste and adjust seasoning if necessary.

This will keep well in the fridge, covered for up to five days.

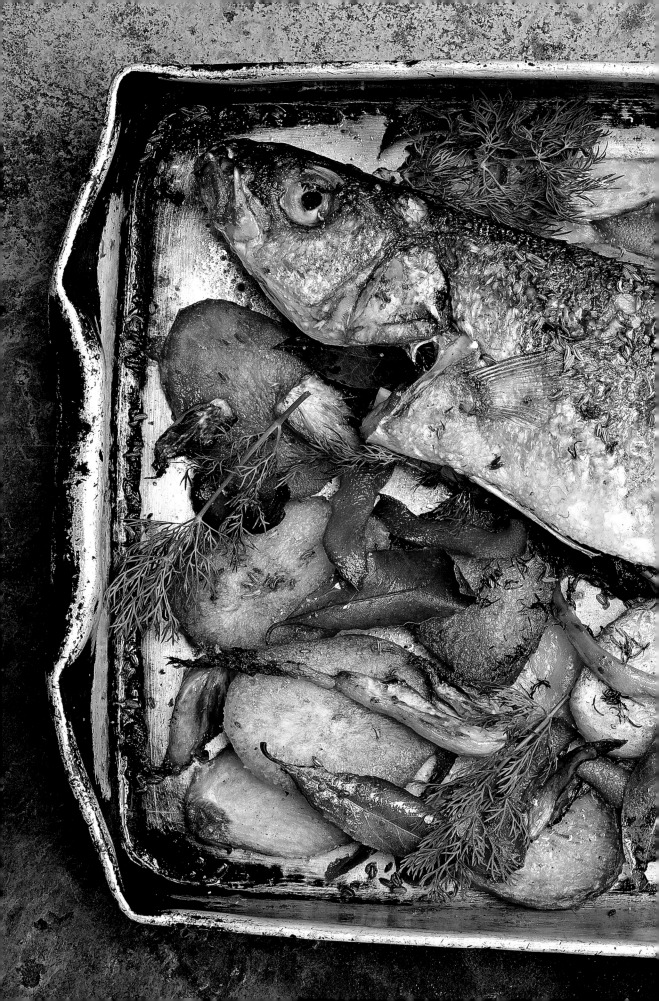

FIG

Originally thought of as a food for the poor — hence the saying 'could not care a fig' — these fruits have become, over the years, rather an extravagent menu item, not found in many restaurants. There is nothing quite like the sight of a French or Italian market stall in the height of late summer. The selection of figs is astounding; from the little pale green ones which can split in two while looking at them, to the long dark purple ones which gently open up at the eye end (osticle) as they ripen, or the small round black ones which taste almost as sweet as a pot of honey. It always suprises me when customers choose the 'perfect looking' fruit over the slightly soft, gooey ones, which often have ripped sides. They are the ones I always head for, being 'perfect' in another sense — ready for eating. To leave them any longer would be a sin.

T HERE CANNOT BE many more wonderful flavours than a perfectly ripe fig, torn open and drizzled with olive oil, sea salt and pepper, served with fresh goat curd or a mound of burrata, the exceptionally creamy, rich, divine elder statesman of the buffalo mozzarella family.

In every basket of figs however there are inevitably the ones which are not quite ripe or have not seen their full quota of sun. These are the ones which need a little help to bring out their flavours – either roasted, baked or perhaps chopped and marinated. Here is a perfect recipe for a few less than perfect figs.

FIGS GRILLED WITH GOAT CHEESE, HONEY AND BAYONNE HAM

6 ripe figs, green or purple
300 g soft goat cheese or goat curd
12 slices of Bayonne, Parma or similar
    ham

12 large basil leaves
A little good olive oil
3 tsp honey, warmed until runny
1 tbsp balsamic vinegar

Wash and trim the core end of the figs and cut in half. If using fresh goat cheese, slice thinly.

Lay the slices of ham on a board next to each other. At one end of each, place a piece of fig, a slice of cheese, or a teaspoon of goat curd. Season with salt and pepper, then place a leaf of basil on top. Gently roll up, with the filling neatly tucked inside. Continue in the same way with the remaining ingredients. Place in the fridge, covered, and chill for up to an hour.

PREHEAT THE GRILL OR OVEN TO 175°C
Place the ham rolls, well-spaced, on a baking sheet, drizzle with a little olive oil and bake or grill until the ham starts to crisp at the edges and the cheese starts to soften.

With tongs remove carefully to a serving platter, drizzle with honey and a drop or two of good quality balsamic vinegar. Serve immediately with Focaccia (page 251) or Spiced Seeded Flat Bread (page 128).

SPICED SEEDED FLAT BREAD

10 g fresh yeast (or 5 g dry or 2.5 g easy-blend)

70 ml olive oil, plus extra for brushing

140 ml warm water

300 g strong white flour

½ tsp chopped thyme

15 g salt

A scant amount of fresh chopped chilli

1 egg white, whisked well with a pinch of salt

A few nigella seeds or fennel seeds

Salt

If using fresh yeast, mix with the olive oil and water until smooth. Cover and allow to prove in a warm place for up to 20 minutes. If using dry or easy-blend yeast simply mix the olive oil and water together. Mix the flour (and the dry or easy-blend yeast if using) together with the chopped thyme, salt and chopped chilli. Stir in the liquids and mix either by hand, or in a mixer with the dough hook attachment on a slow speed, until the dough has become smooth, soft and elastic (approximately 5–7 minutes). Leave covered in a warm place to prove again, for up to 1 hour, during which time it will almost double in size.

PREHEAT THE OVEN TO 180°C

Brush two baking sheets with olive oil.

Cut the dough into 6 or 8 equal-sized pieces and using a pasta rolling machine, or a rolling pin with a dusting of flour, roll the dough into long strips approximately 6cm wide, and long enough to fit the baking sheets. The pasta machine will need to be adjusted down to an increasingly narrow aperture until a long wide strip of dough has been created.

Lay the strips of dough side by side, brush gently with the egg white, sprinkle with the seeds and salt and allow to rest for a few minutes before baking.

Bake for 12–15 minutes or until crisp and golden. Remove to a cooling tray.

Serve with soups, salads, hummus or soft cheeses.

T HE MOST SIMPLE, and the most delicious, of dishes – prepare this as close to the serving time as possible. If this is not possible, cover the plated sliced figs tightly and leave in the fridge for up to an hour before finishing with the remaining ingredients.

FIGS WITH BALSAMIC VINEGAR, CHIVE BLOSSOMS AND SHAVED PARMESAN

8 large ripe figs, green or black
4 tbsp olive oil
2 tbsp balsamic vinegar
Salt and pepper
1 tbsp chopped chives
A few handfuls of small salad leaves, washed

100 g shaved Parmesan or Spenwood
1 tbsp long chopped chives and their blossoms, or nasturtium blossoms if available

Wash and trim the core end of the figs and slice from top to bottom into 3 or 4 pieces depending on the size. Lay them slightly overlapping on a plain serving dish.

Mix together the olive oil, balsamic vinegar, salt, pepper and chopped chives.

Scatter a few small salad leaves over the figs (landcress, watercress, rocket leaves are best), then drizzle with some of the dressing. Place the shavings of cheese decoratively over, then the long chives and snip the chive blossoms on top or place the nasturtium blossoms decoratively around.

Serve any remaining dressing separately.

FIG, ALMOND AND STRAWBERRY TARTLETS WITH BROWN SUGAR

250 g puff pastry
80 g caster sugar
80 g soft butter
A few drops of vanilla extract
80 g ground almonds
Pinch salt
1 egg, whisked

6 large medium-ripe figs
50 g Demerara sugar
350 g strawberries
250 g mascarpone
50 ml double cream
1 tbsp Demerara sugar
Icing sugar for dusting

Roll the puff pastry very thinly into a rectangle approximately 50 cm x 30 cm and chill on a parchment-lined baking sheet in the fridge or freezer for up to an hour. Beat the caster sugar, butter and vanilla until very pale, gently fold in the ground almonds and salt until amalgamated, then add the whisked egg, beating until smooth.

PREHEAT THE OVEN TO 200°C

Trim the figs and cut into quarters or sixths. Cut the pastry into 6 12–15 cm discs and prick the centre of each one a few times with a fork, leaving a 2 cm rim around the edge. Spread the almond mixture over the centre of each disc, place the figs on top, skin sides down, pressing into the mixture. Sprinkle with 25 g of the Demerara sugar.

Gently crimp the rim of the pastry until each tartlet has a shallow ridge around the edge. Brush the rims with a tiny amount of water and sprinkle with a little of the Demerara sugar. Bake the tartlets for 15 minutes or until the pastry edges colour. Turn the temperature to 170°c and cook for a further 25 minutes or until the pastry is cooked through thoroughly and the almond mixture set and golden.

Hull and halve or quarter the strawberries, place in a bowl with the remaining Demerara sugar and toss gently. Whip the mascarpone with the cream and the tablespoon of Demerara sugar until light and smooth. Allow the tartlets to cool a little before scattering the strawberries over, filling the gaps between the baked figs. Serve, dusted with icing sugar, with the mascarpone cream on the side.

ONE OF THE highlights of my restaurant's 30th anniversary year was when Alice Waters and I co-hosted a week-long series of Chez Panisse-inspired celebratory lunches and dinners. I could never have done this event justice, or made it even close to perfection, without the support and help of two wonderful cooks, David Lindsey and Claire Ptak. Each morning we would discuss the day's menus and plan our work ahead. They were the dream team for me and I felt so happy and relaxed to leave them in charge of my kitchen.

Claire took over the running of the pastry section and, together with my team, created the most wonderful desserts, including individual baked Alaskas, baked elderberries with quince, and roasted purple Italian figs which were at the peak of their season that month. With these, she served a fragrant ice cream made with toasted fig leaves, which I had picked from a friend's garden in Kensington Church Street that morning.

Claire has very kindly allowed me to reproduce her recipe here, from her delectable book *The Violet Bakery Cookbook* published by Square Peg, and reproduced by permission of The Random House Group Ltd.

FIG LEAF ICE CREAM

---

10 new spring fig leaves
350 ml whole milk
175 g caster sugar

4 egg yolks
650 ml double cream

PREHEAT THE GRILL
Lay the fig leaves out flat on a baking tray.

Place the tray on the highest rack in your grill and leave the door ajar. After a few minutes you will start to smell the wonderful heady aroma of the fig leaves warming up and then starting to singe under the flame. Let them take on a little bit of colour before you take them out.

In a heavy-bottomed pan, warm the milk, sugar and fig leaves until just beginning to bubble. This won't take too long, so while it's heating up, put your egg yolks into a bowl and whisk to break them up. Measure the double cream into a large container or bowl and set aside.

When the milk is ready, temper the yolks by pouring a little of the milk into them, whisking as you go. Now pour the tempered yolks back into the remaining warm milk in the pan. Stirring continuously, heat until the mixture starts to thicken at the bottom of the pan, checking it now and again by bringing your stirring spoon up out of the pan.

Pour the custard mixture into the cold cream and whisk well to prevent the custard from cooking any further. Cover and put in the fridge for a least an hour to cool. Once the ice cream base has cooled, pour it through a fine sieve to remove the leaves and any eggy bits. Pour into your ice cream machine and churn for about 20 minutes, following the manufacturer's instructions. Freeze for an hour before serving. This will keep for 3 to 4 days in the freezer before it starts to get icy.

LANDCRESS

Probably my favourite salad, this peppery leaf is not so easy to find and to some is an acquired taste. Its closest cousin, watercress, both the green and the slightly unusual red, are much more common, and can be found in vegetable shops and supermarkets most of the year round, often imported from France. In season of course, the UK farmers' markets will offer all types of cress and the following recipes could contain a combination of all three types if you are lucky enough to find them.

As Tessa's beautiful photograph shows it grows a little like a star fish, spreading its branches over and across the earth. The leaves are rounded and the older the plant becomes the more leaves appear on each stem. It is much more peppery than watercress and should there-fore be used with care, possibly tossed with other, slightly more neutral leaves to give a balance to the dish.

SCALLOP CEVICHE WITH
LANDCRESS, LIME AND CHILLI

100 g landcress or 1 large bunch
  watercress
12 medium-large diver-caught scallops,
  out of the shell
Juice of 2 limes

1 lime, cut into 6 wedges
1 small red chilli finely chopped,
  without seeds
3 tbsp olive oil
Salt

Pick through the landcress or watercress, removing tough stalks and discoloured leaves. Rinse carefully in cold water and spin gently in a salad spinner. Wrap in damp kitchen paper and place in the fridge until required.

Remove the muscle from the side of each scallop and discard. Remove the roe from each scallop and retain for another use.

Rinse the scallops in very cold water to remove any sand or grit and pat dry with kitchen paper. Lay on a dish, cover tightly with clingwrap and chill in the fridge for up to an hour, until very firm.

Placing the scallops one by one on a board, circumference down-wards and using a small sharp knife, slice each as thinly as possible, and place directly onto a baking sheet lined with clingwrap. (The slicing is made easier by freezing the scallops for a few minutes first.)

Add the chopped chilli to the lime juice little by little until the level of piquancy is to your taste. With a small spoon sprinkle the juice over the scallops evenly. Cover with clingwrap and chill for up to three hours. To serve, remove the clingwrap and use a spoon to lift the scallops and juices onto six plates, spreading them evenly and attractively across the plates. Scatter the landcress all over, drizzle with olive oil and sprinkle with salt. Garnish with lime wedges and serve with buttered brown bread.

I F I HAD to choose my favourite meal it would indeed include crab in some shape or form. Freshly cooked, picked and served simply with a squeeze of lemon it can be sublime. However these little spicy crab cakes, fried just before serving, can easily come a close second.

CRAB CAKES WITH LANDCRESS, CHILLI, CREME FRAICHE AND LIME

400g freshly picked white crab meat
200g freshly picked brown crab meat
300g potatoes, peeled and washed
1 sweetcorn
2 tbsp chopped chives or spring onion
   tops
2 tbsp chopped coriander leaves
Salt
½ green chilli, finely chopped
Juice of 1 lime
1 tbsp lemon mayonnaise (page 32),
   or soured cream or crème fraîche

A little flour
2 eggs, whisked with a little salt
Dried breadcrumbs — see below

To serve :
Crème fraîche or soured cream
1 lime, cut into wedges
Landcress or watercress picked, washed
   and spun
Coriander sprigs

Check the crab for stray pieces of shell or cartilage and leave covered in the fridge until required. Crab must stay cold at each stage of its preparation as it is one of the most vulnerable foods and can turn very easily.

Cook the potatoes in boiling salted water until tender, then strain and cover with a tea towel for a few minutes to absorb the steam as they cool.

Meanwhile remove the husk and hairs from the sweetcorn, remove the kernels with a sharp knife and cook for a few minutes until tender in a small amount of boiling salted water. Drain and cool.

Mash the potatoes using a potato masher or ricer, and place in a bowl with the corn, herbs, salt and chilli.

Mix the two crab meats into the mash until well blended, add the lime juice and enough mayonnaise or cream to bind the mixture together. It should be firm enough to hold its shape but soft enough to scoop easily. Taste and adjust the seasoning if necessary. With a dessert spoon scoop into 12 little patties and place onto a baking sheet. Cover and chill for at least an hour. Meanwhile, make the dried breadcrumbs.

TO MAKE THE DRIED BREADCRUMBS

Preheat the oven to 170°c. Cut some, though not all the crusts from a loaf of a plain bread and discard – ideally the bread should not contain too much olive oil or herbs as these will burn easily.

Cut the bread into small chunks and process little by little in a food processor, until it resembles rough crumbs. Spread out over one or two baking sheets and bake in the oven until golden (approximately 10–15 minutes).

Allow to cool before reprocessing in the food processor until fine. Stored chilled in an airtight container these crumbs will last for up to three weeks, or will freeze beautifully.

TO FINISH THE CRAB CAKES

Using a little flour, to prevent sticking, shape each crab cake into a ball or a flattish patty. Leave on the tray.

Place the egg wash and breadcrumbs in two medium-sized bowls next to each other.

Using one hand for the egg and one for the crumbs, dip the crab cake first into the egg and then into the crumbs, making sure that the surfaces are entirely coated and sealed. Cover and chill until required.

PREHEAT THE OVEN TO 170°C

In a heavy-based frying pan, heat ½ cm vegetable oil until a bread-crumb sizzles readily.

Place a few crab cakes in the oil at a time, fry until golden-brown (approximately 1–2 minutes), then turn over carefully to cook the other side. Place in the oven, on a baking sheet lined with lots of kitchen paper, to keep warm while the remainder are fried. Serve as soon as possible with a pot of crème fraîche or soured cream on the side, wedges of lime, landcress leaves and coriander sprigs to scatter.

WHEN I WAS young my mother used to make little sandwiches for tea during term time, for my brothers and me.
I knew no other mother who made them quite as she did
– and certainly it would be frowned upon today. White sliced bread,
buttered generously, filled with crisp salad leaves and sprinkled with
granulated sugar! Our frayed nerves and depleted energy levels were
soon swapped for smiles and keenness to embark on homework after
one or two of them.

Perhaps this sandwich, whilst not immediately appealing to young
children, is a little more up to date in style and more appropriate for
the health-conscious.

LANDCRESS AND LEMON
MAYONNAISE SANDWICHES WITH
NASTURTIUM BLOSSOMS

1 large bunch landcress or watercress
Nasturtium leaves and blossoms
 (if available)
6 large slices of granary or wholewheat
 bread

3 large tbsp mayonnaise (page 32)
150 g good quality Cheddar cheese,
 finely sliced or
200 g good quality flaked canned tuna,
 or sardine fillets, or 12 slices of ham

Remove the large stems and discoloured leaves from the salad leaves,
wash the rest and spin dry carefully. Leave the nasturtium blossoms
for garnish.

Lay the bread on a board and spread generously with the mayonnaise.

Scatter the landcress and nasturtium leaves over three of the bread
slices and top with your chosen filling. Place the remaining three slices
on top, mayonnaise side down. Press gently together and wrap tightly
in clingwrap for up to 3 hours. Slice the sandwich crusts off if you
wish, then cut into triangles, squares or rectangles and garnish with
blossoms or extra salad leaves.

LEEK

At the restaurant we use a variety of sizes of leeks for a variety of dishes.

The very young little finger-sized leeks can simply be trimmed top and bottom, rinsed well and the outside leaf removed. These are then blanched for seconds with other spring vegetables such as peas, young carrots, broad beans and spring cabbage. Simply strained and tossed together with olive oil, salt and pepper, they create a perfect bed for a poached fish fillet or chicken breast for example.

The slightly thicker 'teenage' leeks (as we call them) are lovely prepared, cooked and served in the same way, but I almost prefer them grilled with olive oil and sea salt or roasted for a few minutes and served warm or chilled with a salad of crumbled ricotta, pine nuts and a drizzle of aged balsamic vinegar.

LEEK, WHITE BEAN AND HAM SOUP

250 g dried cannellini or borlotti beans
600 g fresh ham hock
1 medium onion, peeled and quartered,
    root on
2 sticks celery, washed and sliced
A few springs rosemary, thyme, bay and
    parsley, tied together
2 cloves garlic, gently crushed
1 carrot, peeled and cut lengthwise
Salt

2 tbsp olive oil

To finish the broth:
3 tbsp olive oil
1 clove garlic, crushed
1 tsp chopped thyme
2 large leeks, trimmed, washed well and
    sliced
1 tbsp chopped celery leaves
1 tbsp chopped parsley leaves

Soak the dried beans overnight in lots of cold water.

The following day bring the beans to the boil in fresh water, drain, rinse and place in a clean pan with the ham hock, onion, celery, herbs, garlic and carrot. Cover well with cold water and bring to the boil. Simmer gently (adding extra water if the level diminishes) for up to an hour, or until the beans are tender throughout. Remove the pieces of vegetable and the herbs with tongs.

Remove the hock piece and trim off excess fat, then dice the meat finely.

In a large heavy-based pan heat the olive oil, crushed garlic and thyme until fragrant, add the leeks and cook until soft but not coloured. Add the ham and then the beans including the broth. Bring to the boil, taste and adjust seasoning. Add chopped celery and parsley leaves and serve drizzled with extra olive oil.

LEEK VINAIGRETTE WITH CHOPPED EGG, CHIVES AND MUSTARD DRESSING

6 small leeks
2 tsp Dijon mustard
2 tbsp wine vinegar
Salt and pepper
5 tbsp light olive oil

3 eggs
1 tbsp long chopped chives
1 tbsp small capers
2 tbsp roughly chopped parsley

Choose even-sized small (not baby) leeks, trim away the dark green ends and peel off the outside layers. Rinse, cut in half lengthwise and rinse again very well. Cut each half to the same length, approximately 10 cm. Use the trimmings for soup or stock.

To make the dressing, whisk the mustard with the wine vinegar, salt, pepper and light olive oil.

Hard boil the eggs by placing them in a small pan, covering with cold water and bringing them to the boil. Cook for 7 minutes then rapidly cool them under cold running water. Peel and cut open the eggs, remove the yolks and crumble or push through a wide-gauged sieve. Chop the egg white roughly.

Bring a pan of salted water to the boil and cook the leeks gently until tender. Drain carefully and remove them to a serving platter, lining them next to each other, cut sides up. Pour the dressing over the warm leeks and leave to cool.

To serve, scatter the egg white over, then the yolk, then finish with lots of chives, capers and parsley.

A lovely dish to serve with cold sliced ham, or as part of a selection of old fashioned hors d'oeuvres.

SMOKED HADDOCK AND LEEK PASTIES

600 ml milk

2 bay leaves

A few sprigs dill and thyme

½ tsp crushed peppercorns

600 g smoked haddock, bones removed, and cut into 2 or 3 pieces

100 g butter

2 medium leeks, washed and finely sliced

3 sticks celery, washed and finely sliced

2 tbsp chopped dill, plus ½ tbsp chopped dill for finishing

Salt and pepper

30 g flour

500 g puff pastry

1 egg, whisked with a little salt for wash

In a wide pan bring the milk to a gentle simmer with the bay leaves, herb sprigs and crushed peppercorns and leave covered, off the heat, for 15 minutes. Place the haddock in the infused milk over a medium heat. Poach gently for 7–10 minutes or until the fish flakes easily. Remove from the heat and cool the fish in the liquid. Remove the skin carefully from the fish, break the haddock into large flakes, strain the liquid and discard the debris. There should be approximately 300 ml milk after cooking.

In a heavy-based pan heat half the butter, add the leek and celery and cook without colouring until soft. Season with salt, pepper and 2 tablespoons of the chopped dill, remove with a slotted spoon and add to the fish.

Add the remaining butter to the pan and cook over a medium heat with the flour, without colouring, for 1 minute. Slowly add the warm infused milk stirring continuously until the sauce thickens – approximately 3 minutes.

Add the sauce to the fish, stir gently until well amalgamated and allow to cool. Chill in the fridge for up to 24 hours.

Roll the puff pastry into a large rectangle, approximately 45 cm x 30 cm and cut into 6 squares. If it becomes difficult to handle, place in the fridge to chill.

Lay the 6 pieces of pastry side by side and divide the chilled fish mixture between them, placing onto the centre of each piece. Brush the edges with egg wash and seal the edges together, making a triangular shape. Crimp the edges decoratively.

Brush the pastry with the remaining egg wash and sprinkle with the remaining dill and a little salt. Ideally chill for 1 hour before baking.

PREHEAT THE OVEN TO 200°C

Lay the pasties on a baking sheet lined with parchment paper and bake for 20 minutes or until the pastry is golden. Turn the oven down to 180°C and cook for a further 10 minutes until piping hot throughout.

Serve warm or straight from the oven – or chilled they make a lovely addition to a picnic.

LEMON AND LIME

I love the look of the first unwaxed, untreated lemons which arrive in late spring from Italy, often with their leaves and branches still attached. Immediately I put them in the shop for display, for the customers to admire and purchase, and for the cooks to collect when needed. They remind me of the gardens and restaurants of the Amalfi coast, which are full to overflowing with citrus fruit trees in the early part of the year. Lemons, oranges, limes, tangerines and citron (limone pane) which resemble huge thick skinned lemons, the size of melons. A friend in Naples has them lying in dishes around his apartment, to give the most delicious scent to the rooms.

For the rest of the year, as lemons and limes are needed in so many dishes, for use in so many ways, I have over time, bent the 'eat locally-sourced' rule in the winter months when one craves a few fresh, astringent flavours to liven up the taste buds.

WHEN I THINK of my early days in California, I think of the smells. The eucalyptus trees in the woods and by the road sides; the mesquite wood-smoke of barbecues in the Malibu hills and of the oil from the zests of lime, as the wedges were squeezed over gin and tonics, Bloody Marys and into bowls of guacamole.

Coriander was used infrequently in my household before my travels to America, but because of the south-western state's close proximity to Latin America and its Hispanic immigrant population, I grew to know and love the herb, and still use it in some way, in some dish, almost every day at the restaurant.

Apparently, to some taste buds, coriander has a 'soapy' flavour, a flavour that masks others in a detrimental way. I strongly disagree, and try hard to promote it within our menus, and by doing this, hope to gently persuade the 'antis' over to my camp.

This recipe is so simple and so quick to assemble – and takes me back to my second home, California.

SALAD OF AVOCADO, VINE TOMATOES, LIME AND CORIANDER

2–3 large avocados
650 g ripe cherry, plum or heritage
   tomatoes
Juice of 3 limes
1 lime, cut into wedges
½ small bunch coriander
4 tbsp olive oil

Salt
½ long red chilli, finely chopped
1 small red onion, peeled
A few lettuces such as escarole, garden
   rocket, mizuna, oak leaf or little gem,
   washed and spun dry
1 tbsp chopped chives

Choose ripe but firm avocados, ripe and juicy vine tomatoes of any shape or colour. Pick the coriander sprigs and leaves from the stems into iced water, dry them carefully with kitchen paper. Keep the sprigs separate for garnish.

Wash and core the large tomatoes and cut all into even-sized pieces – either into wedges, halves or slices, depending on their size and shape. Place into a bowl and sprinkle with half the lime juice, olive oil, salt and the chopped chilli. Toss gently together.

Cut the avocados in half, remove the stones and peel. Slice into large wedges and arrange on a serving platter. Pour the remaining lime juice over and around, drizzle with olive oil and sea salt. Cut the red onion in half, remove the tough outer layers, and slice into paper thin slices creating half-moons.

Tear the lettuces carefully into even-sized pieces and toss into the tomatoes with the coriander leaves (not sprigs), sliced onion and chives.

Pile this on top of the avocado (it is best not to jumble the avocado in as well as the pieces are likely to break up and spoil the appearance).

Finish with sprigs of coriander, wedges of lime and serve immediately with warm Spiced Seeded Flat Bread (page 128), grilled chicken, hamburgers, slices of mozzarella or young goat cheese.

LEMON AND LIME ICE CREAM

Juice and zest of 1 lemon
Juice and zest of 3 limes
250 ml milk

80 g sugar
4 egg yolks
250 ml double cream

Bring the milk to the boil, add both the zests, cover and leave off the heat to infuse for up to an hour. Whisk the sugar and yolks together until pale, add the milk and pour back into the pan. Stir over medium heat, stirring continuously until it thickens. Do not allow to boil; allow the eggs to thicken the custard gently and gradually. Strain into a bowl over a larger bowl of iced water to stop the cooking immediately and prevent curdling. Add the citrus juices and double cream, taste and churn in an ice cream machine, following the manufacturer's instructions. Scoop into a freezer container with a lid and serve, ideally within 24 hours, although it will last to up to two weeks if required. Serve with Puff Pastry Twists and Sugared Candied Peel (page 160).

PUFF PASTRY TWISTS

200 g puff pastry
1 egg white whisked

60 g caster sugar, mixed with
½ tsp cinnamon

Roll the pastry to approximately 3–5 mm thick and chill in a fridge or freezer for a minimum of 1 hour. Line two baking sheets with silicone wax paper.

Place the pastry on a chopping board, brush with the whisked egg white and sprinkle generously with the cinnamon sugar. Using the rolling pin, press the sugar gently into the egg. Using a long sharp knife and working quickly (as the pastry needs to stay cool), cut it into strips approximately 1 cm wide.

Pick one strip up at a time and twist it to resemble a screw. Lay them on the baking sheets, leaving a little space between them. Chill again for a few minutes while preheating the oven to 175°C. Bake for 10–12 minutes or until crisp and golden. Remove to a cooling rack and serve within 24 hours.

L IMES AND PASSION fruit are two ingredients which partner each other so perfectly and this little tartlet is a real tongue-zapper. It is often on the restaurant menus during the winter months.

LIME AND PASSION FRUIT MERINGUE TARTLETS

For the pastry:
90 g butter, chilled and cubed
180 g plain flour
Pinch salt
60 g caster sugar
1 egg yolk, whisked with a splash of water
Dried beans for the baking

For the curd:
6 egg yolks (only 4 of the whites to be used for meringue)

100 g caster sugar
Peelings of 2 limes
Juice of 4 limes, approximately 150 ml
5 passion fruit, squeezed, including seeds
100 g soft unsalted butter, cut into small pieces

For the meringue:
Reserved egg whites
Pinch of salt
300 g caster sugar

FOR THE PASTRY

Rub the butter into the flour and salt with cool fingers until it resembles breadcrumbs. Add the sugar, the egg yolk whisked with water, and knead the dough gently together. Add a little more water or flour if it seems too dry or too wet. Shape it into a thick log and chill for up to an hour. Cut into 6 equally sized pieces and roll each one with a light dusting of flour into a thin disc approximately 18 cm across and 5 mm thick.

Line 6 tartlet tins, of 10 cm diameter and 2 cm deep, pressing the dough carefully into the corners at the base.

Chill again for 20–30 minutes then line with discs of parchment paper and fill with baking beans.

PREHEAT THE OVEN TO 175°C

Bake for 20 minutes or until the pastry is golden brown at the edges. Carefully remove the papers and continue to bake the pastry for a further 5 minutes or until the bases of the pastry are cooked through.

Separate the eggs, keeping four of the whites for the meringue.

Mix the yolks with the sugar, lime juice, lime peelings and passion fruit in a medium bowl until well blended. Place the bowl over a pan of gently simmering water on a low heat and stir continuously with a wooden spoon until it begins to thicken. When it is thick enough to coat the back of the spoon remove from the heat and stir in the butter until it has melted. Through a medium gauge sieve, strain into a clean bowl and leave to cool. Discard the seeds and peelings.

FOR THE MERINGUE

Using a clean bowl and a clean, dry whisk, whisk the 4 whites with a pinch of salt until soft peaks are formed. Add half the sugar and continue to whisk until stiff peaks are formed. Fold in the remaining sugar and place in a piping bag with a wide nozzle.

PREHEAT THE OVEN TO 150°C

Divide the curd between the tartlets, flattening the top of each a little. Pipe or spoon the meringue on top decoratively, filling to the edges. Sprinkle with a little extra caster sugar.

Place in the oven and bake for 30 minutes or until the meringue is crisp but not coloured – it should remain marshmallowy inside.

Serve warm or chilled with whipped cream.

C ANDYING PEEL REQUIRES six days. The first day needs the most time, then you must allow a little time each day to complete the process.

CANDIED CITRUS PEEL

Approximately 6 large oranges or 12 large lemons, washed

400 g granulated sugar
50 g glucose syrup

Choose oranges or lemons with thick skins, and ideally either from an organic source or from a producer who grows them naturally, without waxing or treatment.

Score the peel in quarters, from top to bottom. Pull the peel away from the fruit, including all the pith, as this is the main point of candied peel. Place into a stainless steel pan, cover with water and bring to the boil. Simmer for 30 minutes until soft. Drain, leaving the peel in the pan.

Place 250 g of the sugar into the pan and just enough water to cover. Bring gently to a boil as the sugar dissolves, then simmer for 30 minutes. Leave to cool with the lid on.

The next day, strain the syrup into a small stainless steel pan, add 50 g of the remaining sugar, dissolve gently as before and then bring to the boil. Pour this syrup back over the peel, cover and allow to cool, then leave to soak for 24 hours.

Repeat the process twice more, each time adding 50 g more sugar to the syrup.

On the fifth day add the glucose syrup instead, bring to the boil, pour over the peel and leave to cool. Keep it well covered by gently pressing the peel under the syrup, possibly using a small plate pressed down inside the pan.

After a further 24 hours, the peel will be perfectly candied and ready for use. A long process I know, but well worth the effort.

FOR SUGARED CANDIED PEEL
Remove a few pieces of the candied peel from the syrup and pat dry with kitchen paper. Trim any irregular sides away and use for another

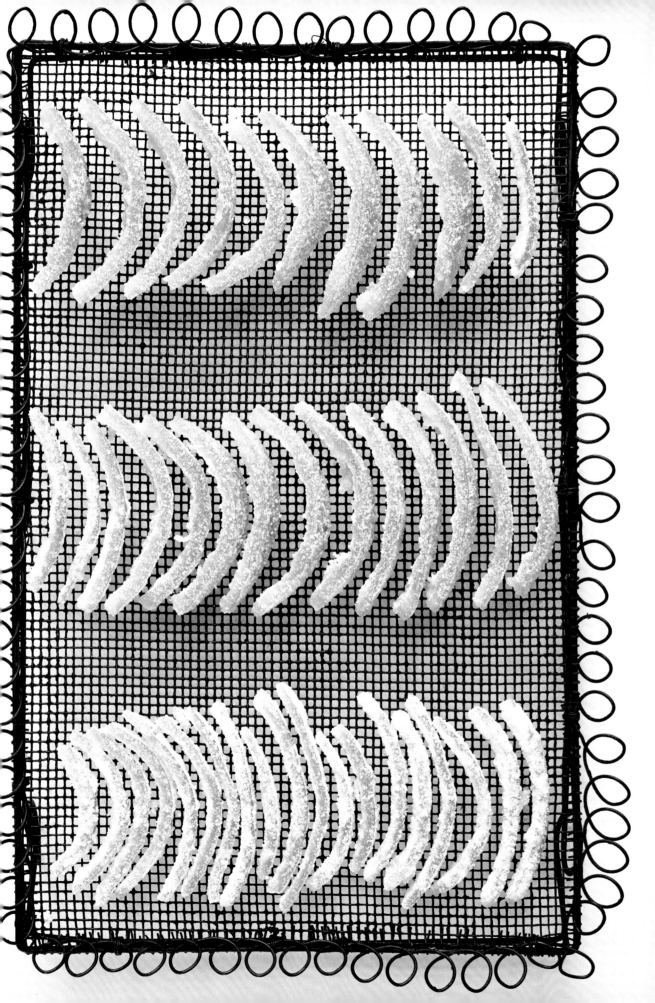

recipe (for example Lemon and Brown Sugar Shortbread page 163).

Slice the peel into fine even-sized strips. Cover a small plate with fine layer of sugar and one by one, press the strips into the sugar, turn over and repeat. Lay the sugared peel on a cooling rack and allow to dry slowly over a day or two, in a cool airy place. Once dry and firm, they will keep in an airtight container for up to a month.

Eat with after-dinner coffee or as an accompaniment to ice creams, syllabubs or fruit fools.

LEMON AND BROWN SUGAR
SHORTBREAD

125 g very soft unsalted butter
75 g soft light brown sugar
225 g plain flour
Zest of 1 large lemon, finely chopped

60 g candied lemon peel, finely chopped
(optional, page 160)
Approximately 2 tbsp Demerara sugar

In a mixing bowl whisk the butter and sugar until light and fluffy. Mix in the flour, zest and candied peel if using, gently but thoroughly.

Roll into a log approximately 2–3 cms in diameter, and then roll this in the Demerara sugar until the surface has a fine coating of sugar.

Wrap in clingwrap and chill until firm.

PREHEAT THE OVEN TO 150°C
Using a heavy sharp knife, slice into discs approximately ½ cm thick, and lay, cut sides down, on a baking sheet lined with parchment paper, leaving space around each one as they will spread a little.

Bake for approximately 20 minutes or until pale and golden. Turn the tray halfway through to ensure even baking. Allow to cool for a few moments, store in an airtight container and eat within four days – although they will probably disappear within minutes!

OLIVE

I do not think an hour passes in our kitchens that does not include the use of olive oil for something — in fact across the Bakery, Production Kitchen and the Restaurant Kitchen we are probably using it in some form every minute.

I used to have a running bet with another chef in London that we used more olive oil than he did during the week — and I believe we won, because we were also producing olive oil-based breads such as foccacia, fougasse and ciabatta for our shop as well as the restaurant.

Almost all our savoury foods are either dressed in olive oil, cooked in a base of olive oil and herbs, or marinated in olive oil with garlic, chilli or other aromatics. Occasionally we make a most lovely cake using olive oil, to serve with ice creams and poached fruits - the Chez Panisse Sauternes and Olive Oil Cake (Chez Panisse Desserts by Lindsey R Shere).

Over the years we have used many wonderful oils from many parts of the globe, including South Australia, Northern California, Greece, Italy and France — and I still do not have a favourite. I love them all!

Most good kitchens will have two or three olive oils to work with at any time. It is important not to use too extravagant an oil for cooking, as to heat a quality extra virgin olive oil is to spoil it. Most of the recipes in this book require a light olive oil for cooking and as good an oil as you can afford to finish a dish — or to drizzle over a salad or a crostini just before serving.

We choose different olives throughout the year for their shape, colour and texture and offer them at the table for customers to enjoy while choosing their menu.

VEAL WITH SHALLOTS, GREEN OLIVES AND GREMOLATA

1–1.2 kg veal, boned leg or shoulder, trimmed of excess fat

For the marinade:
1 glass white wine
2 cloves garlic, crushed
1 small onion, peeled and finely sliced
1 stick celery, washed and finely chopped
A few bay leaves

To fry the meat:
Light olive oil
Approximately 150 g flour seasoned with salt and pepper

For the stock:
1 stick celery, washed and sliced
1 large carrot, peeled and chopped

1 small onion, peeled and chopped
2 glasses white wine
1 clove garlic, crushed to a cream
A few sage leaves
A few bay leaves
1 glass orange juice
500 ml chicken or veal stock
Salt and pepper

To finish the dish:
6 small shallots, peeled and cut in half
2 medium carrots, peeled and sliced at an angle
2 sticks celery, washed and sliced at an angle
1 tsp chopped sage
A few green olives – preferably Lucques or similar firm green olive

Cut the veal into cubes the size of golf balls and place in a bowl with the marinade. Toss together gently, cover tightly and leave in the fridge overnight.

The following day, drain the meat and dry with kitchen paper. Heat enough olive oil to cover the base of a heavy sauté pan, toss the cubes in the seasoned flour, little by little, and fry in the hot oil until each side is sealed and golden, approximately 1–2 minutes. With a draining spoon, remove to a large ovenproof dish. Continue with the remaining veal in the same way, adding a little extra olive oil if the pan looks dry.

Without rinsing the pan, add a little more olive oil and fry the stock vegetables until starting to colour and soften. Add the wine, garlic, herbs, orange juice and stock and bring to the boil, scraping all the browned pieces from the base of the pan. Tip the entire contents of the pan into the ovenproof dish, over the veal, season with salt and pepper and stir well.

PREHEAT THE OVEN TO 170°C
Bring back to the boil, cover with the lid and place in the oven for 1 hour. Turn the temperature down to 160°C and continue cooking for a further 30 minutes or until the meat feels tender enough to cut with a spoon.

Remove from the oven and carefully remove the meat with tongs to a bowl, strain the juices over and discard the debris. Allow to cool. The meat and juices may be covered and stored in the fridge for up to 48 hours.

Heat the remaining olive oil in a heavy-based pan and add shallots, carrot, and celery and stir until they begin to colour then add the sage. Remove the fat from the surface of the veal and pour the juices over the vegetables. Bring to a simmer and reduce by approximately a third or until the vegetables are soft and the sauce has thickened a little. Add the veal and olives, taste for seasoning and simmer for up to 15 minutes.

Serve with steamed potatoes or rice and then finish with a generous scattering of gremolata.

THIS IS A most magical seasoning – a condiment often used on grilled or braised veal or fish, particularly in Italy. Make within a few hours of serving as the freshness of the ingredients is vital.

GREMOLATA

---

1 small bunch parsley, picked, stalks removed and washed
Zest of 1 lemon, finely grated

1 shallot, peeled and very finely diced
Salt and pepper

Chop the parsley medium-fine. (The volume of parsley should be approximately four times the volume of the lemon and shallot combined.) Mix the ingredients together as close to serving as possible.

MARINATED OLIVES WITH LEMON PEEL, HERBS AND ALMONDS

400 g olives eg Lucques, Niçoise, Kalamata
300 ml olive oil
Peelings of 1 lemon, using a vegetable peeler

A few bay leaves, sprigs of rosemary and thyme
1 tsp coriander seeds
1 tsp fennel seeds
60 g good quality blanched almonds

Choose a variety of olives, small, large, green, black, purple and place in an earthenware pot or glass jar large enough to hold them comfortably.

In a large pan, gently warm the olive oil with the remaining ingredients, and simmer for 2 minutes. Take care as the oil will be hot.

As soon as the aroma of the citrus peel, seeds and herbs is noticeable, remove from the heat with care and pour the entire contents of the pan over the olives. With a wooden spoon, push the infused ingredients in and around the olives.

Allow to cool and store in a cool dark place for up to 3 days.

Drain off excess oil if preferred, and serve the olives with drinks or as an accompaniment to cured meats, soft cheeses, flat bread or toasted ciabatta. Use the fragrant oil for salads, stews and soups.

This recipe will make ample for six people if used with drinks or as part of a first course, but they will keep well if tightly covered in the fridge and then brought to room temperature just before serving.

BLACK OLIVE TAPENADE TOASTS
WITH ANCHOVY AND CAPERS

450 g pitted black olives

6 anchovy fillets in oil

1 clove garlic, crushed to a cream

2 tsp capers, drained of brine or rinsed
    of salt

Zest of 2 lemons, finely grated

1 small chilli, finely chopped

90 ml olive oil

1 tbsp chopped parsley, chives
    and/or thyme

½ baguette

1 clove garlic, cut in half

Chop the olives finely with the anchovy fillets, add the garlic and capers and continue chopping until it becomes a soft paste. Place in a small bowl, taste for seasoning, and add lemon zest, chilli and olive oil until it reaches the consistency you like (stiffer to use as a spread but looser if it is to become a sauce).

Finally add either chopped parsley, chives or thyme – or all three.

This may be made in advance and kept in the fridge – although it is best to add the fresh herbs just before serving.

Slice a baguette (or similar country style bread) thinly and place on a baking sheet, drizzle with olive oil and bake in a medium-hot oven (approximately 180°C) until golden (this may also be done on a char grill – turning over to colour both sides). While still hot, rub each slice with a cut clove of garlic and serve topped with tapenade.

BLOOD ORANGE

Of all the winter fruits, the arrival of the blood oranges from Sicily is the one I relish the most. They usually arrive just in time for Christmas — sometimes only a matter of days beforehand — but the thrill of being able to use the juice, the fruit and the peel in midwinter is exhilarating.

We normally buy from two suppliers — one who finds us the small deep red fleshed oranges which are perfect for juicing and from another, the larger ones which often arrive with their leaves attached, and are flecked inside with splashes of vivid garnet. These we segment both for salads and desserts.

Our freshly-squeezed citrus juices for the bar and shop change throughout the year: pink grapefruit, navel oranges, clementines and then blood oranges if we are lucky, from late November onwards. It is always rather a sad moment when they start to fade and I realise that we will have to wait many months for the new crop to arrive.

PROFESSIONAL CHOCOLATIERS WILL 'temper' their chocolate before using. This involves melting, warming, cooling, adding cold chocolate, warming and cooling again, and is tricky even for the most experienced. The tempering renders the chocolate shiny and bright in appearance and, on setting, it will not lose its allure. Correctly tempered chocolate will last for many weeks if kept at a constantly cool environment; chocolate incorrectly tempered will 'bloom' within a short time, showing patches of white spotting over the surface. Whilst perfectly edible, it is unattractive – and frowned upon by professionals!

The best, most delicious chocolates in the world for me are made by Michael Rechiutti who is based in the Dog Patch region of San Francisco, which is nestled amongst the sprawling bus depots and warehouses of the Bay Area. His modest but impressive workshop creates an ever-changing selection of wonderful chocolates all year round; some filled, some plain, some with biscuit bases and, amongst my favourites, chocolate-dipped wafer-thin slices of oven-dried apples and pears.

Although we produce a lovely variety of chocolates in-house for my shop, I like to import his exquisitely packaged goods for Christmas or Easter. Over the years, he and his wife Jackie have become friends, and their kind advice and encouragement on all things chocolate have been a source of guidance and delight to me.

This little recipe is written in honour of Michael.

CHOCOLATE-DIPPED BLOOD ORANGES

2 ripe but firm blood oranges	300 ml water
200 g granulated sugar	250 g bitter chocolate

Wash the fruit and slice off the top of each. With a fine-bladed sharp knife, slice the fruit as thinly as possible. (A good tip for making this easier is to semi-freeze the fruit for a few moments before slicing. However care should be taken, as the knife could slip dangerously if the fruit becomes too solid.)

Bring the sugar and water to the boil in a wide, heavy-based stainless steel pan. Add the fruit slices and over a low heat, simmer until they are translucent, approximately 5–10 minutes.

PREHEAT THE OVEN TO 160°C

Line two baking sheets with silicone wax paper. Remove the slices from the syrup one by one with a fork or tongs and lay them close but not touching one another on the baking sheets. Retain the syrup for another use.

Bake the slices for 5 minutes then turn off the oven and leave the door slightly ajar. If possible leave them in the oven overnight, or in another warm place until almost dry. Turn them over carefully and air dry for up to an hour or two. (They should remain slightly chewy.)

The next day, chop the chocolate roughly and place in a small bowl. Settle the bowl over a pan of just-boiled water and allow the steam to gently melt the chocolate. Do not let the bowl touch the water – remember chocolate melts in your hand, so gentle steam is all that is necessary.

Line two baking sheets with silicone wax paper. Holding the best edge of each slice between thumb and index finger, dip the other edge (roughly half the surface) in the warm chocolate. Let the excess chocolate drip back into the bowl and place one by one on the paper, leaving a little space between them. Leave in a cool, dry and airy place until firm. Serve ideally within a day, after a meal, with coffee or fresh mint tea.

BLOOD ORANGE ICE CREAM WITH CANDIED ORANGE PEEL

Peelings of 2 blood oranges,
250 ml milk
1 vanilla pod, split lengthwise
400 ml blood orange juice (6–8 blood
  oranges)

4 egg yolks
80 g caster sugar
250 ml cream
75 g candied peel (page 160)

Wash and peel the skin from the 2 oranges with a potato peeler or sharp knife. Remove any pith which may remain on the underside.

Heat the milk gently to a simmer with the orange peelings and split vanilla pod for approximately 5–10 minutes. Cover and remove from the heat, allowing the flavours to infuse for up to 20 minutes. Remove the vanilla pod and, with the back of a knife, scrape the seeds into the milk. (Rinse the empty pod and use for another recipe at a later date.)

Place the measured orange juice in a small stainless steel pan and reduce over a medium-high heat to approximately a third its volume (140 ml).

Whisk the egg yolks and sugar together until thick and creamy, add the milk and continue to stir. Pour into a clean heavy-based pan and stir over a gentle heat until the custard has thickened a little. It should nicely coat the back of a wooden spoon. Do not allow it to scramble – nor take it away from the heat before the egg has become creamy. Strain and then chill over a bowl of ice to arrest the cooking process. Add the cream and reduced blood orange juice and churn in an ice cream machine following the manufacturer's instructions.

Meanwhile trim the candied peel to an even rectangle, cut into fine slices, then cut across into fine dice. As the ice cream is spooned out of the machine, gently fold in the candied peel.

Chill in a freezer until ready to serve – ideally within 24 hours. It will last up to 3–4 weeks in a freezer, although the flavour and texture will diminish over time.

CANDIED PEEL AND ALMOND MACAROONS

200 g ground almonds
300 g caster sugar
30 g flour

4 egg whites
75 g chopped candied orange peel
  (page 160)

Mix the dry ingredients well. In a separate bowl whisk the whites until frothy, not stiff, and add these, little by little, with the candied peel to the almond mix until a soft but not loose, dough is formed. (Not all the whites may be needed.) Cover and chill for a few hours or overnight.

PREHEAT THE OVEN TO 160°C

Line a baking sheet with rice paper or baking parchment. Shape the dough into 12 balls and place on the sheet, with plenty of space between them.

Bake for 20–25 minutes or until lightly golden, crisp on the outside and deliciously soft and chewy on the inside.

THIS SALAD IS vividly red, purple and white – stunning to look at, but difficult to prevent the staining of the various ingredients. It is therefore best assembled just before serving, and instead of making one large salad to share, it is advisable to present individual salads to each guest, and allow them to mess up the look of the plate themselves.

SALAD OF BLOOD ORANGES, BEETROOT AND POMEGRANATE

12 – 18 small or baby beetroots
   (approximately 400 g beetroot)
Salt and pepper
6 blood oranges, plus 1 for juice
60 g hazelnuts
1 large red and 1 large white chicory

1 small green lettuce or 2 little gem or
   a few handfuls of garden rocket or
   young spinach leaves
1 pomegranate
1 tbsp pomegranate molasses (optional)
4 tbsp olive oil
1 tbsp long chopped chives

Wash and trim the beetroot of leaves and any roots which may remain. Cook in simmering salted water, covered with a lid until tender. Cool in the water, peel and cut into small wedges. Marinate in a little olive oil, salt and pepper.

Trim the top and bottom from oranges and then with a small sharp knife trim away the sides in thick 'petals' of peel, which have the merest hint of the orange flesh still attached. In this way the oranges will be peeled to perfection, without a trace of pith. Leave on one side.

In a medium-hot oven, approximately 170°C, roast the hazelnuts until the skins become dark (but not burnt). Rub in a tea towel and discard the skins. Chop or cut the hazelnuts roughly.

Prepare the red and white chicory leaves by removing the roots and trimming away any discoloured parts. Trim the stems from the salad leaves, wash and spin dry.

To deseed the pomegranate, cut it in half across the equator, then knock out the seeds, with a rolling pin or small hammer, over a bowl to catch the juices as well. Pick out the small pieces of cream-coloured membrane and discard.

To make the dressing, drain the pomegranate juices into a small

bowl, add the blood orange juice to this with the pomegranate molasses (if using), salt and pepper and whisk with a fork, adding the olive oil little by little. This will not emulsify as for a mayonnaise, instead it will have a separated look of the ruby red juices melding with the yellow-green of the olive oil.

Slice or segment the oranges, catching any excess juice to add to the dressing.

TO SERVE

Place an assortment of the larger leaves onto each plate. To avoid excessive staining, carefully scatter the blood orange and beetroot over, then finish with the smaller leaves. Sprinkle the pomegranate seeds and chopped hazelnuts over the top and drizzle with a little dressing. Finish with the chopped chives and serve with the remaining dressing separately.

PEA

The first hint that spring is turning a little warmer is when the peas appear in the garden, climbing the bamboo rods and trailing amongst the wild convovulus.

They are arguably best served straight from the garden in the pod, as Fergus Henderson does at St. John Restaurant in London. At the start of the season a bowl of unpodded peas is often placed on the table for customers to share, which not only gives them a talking point but also something to do as they discuss the choices on the menu.

We use them as often as we can during April, May and June, in both starters and main courses. Partnered with green and white asparagus, they make a wonderful fresh salad, tossed gently with watercress or shavings of fennel bulb, then drizzled with a light creme fraiche dressing to finish. A selection of briefly blanched spring vegetables such as carrots, sprouting broccoli and fava beans with freshly podded peas, can become the perfect bed for grilled or poached fish, or roasted spring lamb or chicken.

I S THERE ANYONE in the world who would not like fresh pea soup, served chilled, with a whisper of background notes of mint and spring onion, and a few of the sweetest peas reserved as garnish?

In the winter I like to use butter in most of our soups, or at least a combination of butter and olive oil. It suits the robust nature of big flavoured soups which are often partnered with garlic, root vegetables, meat or fish stocks. However in the summer I find that olive oil is preferable – it offers lightness to the end product and allows the fresh, more delicate flavours to shine through.

CHILLED PEA SOUP WITH MINT, SPRING ONION AND YOGHURT

1.5 kg unpodded peas (500 g podded)
A generous handful of mint stalks
1 bunch spring onions, washed, root ends trimmed
4–6 tbsp olive oil
1 small fennel bulb, washed and roughly chopped
200 g Désirée or King Edward potatoes, washed, peeled and roughly chopped

2 sticks celery, washed and roughly chopped
Small bunch mint leaves
75 g spinach or parsley leaves
170 ml Greek or similar good quality yoghurt
6 small mint sprigs

First make the pea stock: pod the peas and divide them into 2 bowls – the large peas with the medium ones and the tiny peas apart. Reserve the pods, wash them and place in a pan with the mint stalks, barely cover with water (approximately 1.25 litres) and bring to the boil. Simmer for 10–15 minutes or until the stock is flavourful, then strain.

Slice the white part of the spring onions roughly and the green part very finely.

In a heavy-based saucepan heat the olive oil and, over a gentle heat, cook the white part of the spring onion, fennel, potato and celery until just beginning to soften. Do not colour the vegetables – they should simply stew slowly in the oil. Add salt, pepper and a litre of the stock, and simmer until the vegetables are completely soft. Add the large and medium peas and simmer for 3 minutes. Finally add the mint leaves, the spinach or parsley leaves, remove from the heat immediately, and stir together so that the leaves start to wilt. Cool for a few minutes and then place the bulk of the vegetables in a food processor or liquidiser (take care not to overfill the bowl or flask as the contents will still be very warm and therefore dangerous).

Slowly add the liquid from the pan and puree until smooth. Pour through a medium-gauge sieve into a clean container, pushing the debris through with the back of a ladle. Place the container over a bowl of iced water so that the soup chills as quickly as possible. (The quicker this is done, the brighter the green the soup will remain.) Add the remaining pea stock to the soup until the correct consistency is reached – remembering that the soup will thicken on cooling.

Taste and adjust seasoning and chill until ready to serve.

Blanch the small peas in a pan of boiling salted water, strain and chill in iced water, then drain. Add the finely sliced green parts of the spring onion with a touch of olive oil and salt.

TO SERVE

Whip the yoghurt with a little cold water until smooth and the consistency of single cream. Give the soup a good stir and a final taste, pour into six chilled soup plates, drizzle with the yoghurt, sprinkle with the peas and garnish with the mint sprigs.

I ADORE THIS dish and could eat it just by itself, but it usually accompanies poached fish dishes or chicken. Although this recipe does not religiously adhere to the great French classic, it nevertheless shows the peas, the lettuce and the butter at their best.

PETITS POIS A LA FRANCAISE

1 kg unpodded peas (350 g podded), small and medium
1 cos or 3 little gem lettuce
1 white onion, peeled and sliced thinly
1 tsp chopped thyme
100 g butter
Salt and pepper

Pod the peas and use the pods to make 500 ml of pea stock as in the previous recipe.

Trim the root end of the lettuce and discard any discoloured leaves. For the cos, cut and remove the entire root end to release all the leaves. Cut the larger leaves across into 3 or 4 pieces and the smaller leaves in half. The little gems should be cut into quarters or sixths, depending on size, retaining the root end which will keep the leaves attached.

In a wide heavy-based pan, cook the sliced onion and chopped thyme in half the butter over a medium heat until soft and translucent (approximately 5–8 minutes). Add the lettuce and with a wooden spoon, turn the leaves over in the buttery onions. Season with salt and pepper and barely cover with the stock. Cover with a lid and simmer for up to 10 minutes or until the lettuces have wilted down. Add the peas and stir well. Replace the lid and continue to cook until the peas are very soft. Their colour will have faded – but this is part of the romance of this dish.

Turn up the heat, remove the lid and allow some of the juices to evaporate – it should look like a soupy stew. Add the remaining butter, swirl the pan gently so that the juices absorb the richness of the butter. Pour into a beautiful copper dish and serve.

If the stew is chilled immediately, before the final addition of the butter, it may be saved for a day or two hence, but it is far preferable to finish and serve it straight away.

T HIS RECIPE HAS to be made in the spring when both peas and ramsones (wild garlic) are abundant. If wild garlic is not available, young or baby spinach leaves, whilst they will not offer the same striking pungency to the flavour, will, along with the pea puree, add a vivid greenness to the appearance. Remove the pretty white blossoms from the garlic leaves and save until the last second.

PEA RISOTTO WITH WILD GARLIC AND PROSECCO

1 kg unpodded peas (350 g podded)
125 g butter
3 tbsp olive oil
1 medium onion, peeled and finely diced
3 inside sticks of celery, washed and finely sliced
350 g arborio or carnaroli rice
250 ml Prosecco

Salt and pepper
100 g wild garlic (ideally including the blossoms), washed, trimmed of excess stem and sliced into wide ribbons
250 g soft goat cheese
75 g freshly grated Parmesan

Pod the peas and divide them roughly in half – the small ones and the larger ones. Make a stock as on page 185 with the pea pods, using at least 1 litre of water for the cooking.

Place the larger peas in a small pan with a little water and salt. Cook until very soft and either puree with a handheld liquidiser or pass through a medium-gauge sieve. Cool over a bowl of iced water, which will help to retain the brightness of colour, and leave aside.

In a heavy-based pan heat half the butter and all the olive oil until warm, add the onion and celery and cook slowly over a medium heat until they start to lose their crispness. Add the rice and stir continuously over the heat until the oils have been absorbed, approximately 4–5 minutes. Pour the Prosecco into the pan and continue to stir until the liquid has been absorbed, then season with salt and pepper.

Strain the warm stock and add this little by little with a ladle to the rice, stirring each time a ladleful is added, and waiting until the liquid has been absorbed before adding the next. The risotto will be cooked within 15–20 minutes and will need approximately 500 ml of the stock.

Keep checking the texture of the rice during the cooking (it should retain a little firmness to the bite, but be pleasantly chewy at the same time).

Five minutes before it is ready, add the raw peas and a little more stock – the peas will cook better in a liquid risotto.

Continue stirring while the risotto finishes cooking, finally adding the garlic leaves and pea puree (which will make the risotto turn a brilliant green) just before it is taken off the heat, allowing the leaves time to wilt into the cooked rice. Remove from the heat when the consistency is to your liking – ideally not too soupy, though not at all solid.

Gently stir the goat cheese and the remaining butter into the risotto and leave covered for a few minutes before serving in warm soup bowls or plates, scattered with freshly grated Parmesan and the reserved wild garlic blossoms.

PEACH

How versatile is the peach. And how many there are — from yellow and white peaches, to flat-bottomed, to wine peaches which, when cut open, show a stunningly beautiful red-stained flesh.

But no matter which one you choose, it has to be perfectly ripe to be really enjoyed. I often feel that the French and Italian growers save the best peaches for themselves and send the second class fruits to Britain, as I know how perfect the fruits are when I choose them from their market stalls in the summer. But of course it is a matter of transport. To carry a perfect peach from one country to another without damaging it is nigh on impossible. It needs a little firmness to stay safe, so it has to be picked early, before it has fully ripened, then packed into crates lined with straw or plastic trays. It therefore 'ripens' during its journey, not on the branch — not natural and not ideal. However, we receive our stone fruits from the continent from as early as May and at the restaurant it serves as one of our first indications that summer is just around the corner.

ALMOST EVERY TIME I eat at Chez Panisse there is a galette on the dessert menu – made with figs or apples or, perhaps one of my favourites, the pluot, a wonderful fruit which I have only ever found in California. It is a cross between an apricot and a dark plum – firm enough to slice and bake, yet soft enough to 'give', making it a perfect eating fruit as well.

The pastry which Chez Panisse uses for its sweet open galette-style tart is similar to our rough puff pastry that everyone used to learn at school. The flour is rubbed into the butter and vice versa but not so finely as for a sweet pastry or shortcrust. The lumps of butter should still be visible when the pastry is brought together with the iced water, and again when rolled out. In this way, the lightness and flakiness of the dough is retained, and when cooked should look both rough and puffed.

In this recipe I have used peaches which are cooked within the part-baked pastry, then it is finished with the fresh raspberries, but any fruit in any season may be used as a substitute depending on the time of year.

PEACH AND RASPBERRY GALETTE

150 g flour	500 g ripe peaches
Pinch fine salt	50 g caster sugar
1 tsp caster sugar	225 g raspberries
75 g soft unsalted butter	Icing sugar for dusting

Sieve the flour, salt and sugar into a bowl and add the soft butter in scoops. With cold fingers, gently rub the ingredients together until most, but not all, of the butter has been blended into the flour. Bring the dough together with a little iced water, scrape the sides of the bowl and bring the mass together gently with floured hands. Wrap with clingwrap and leave in the fridge for up to 2 hours to chill.

Flour the work surface lightly and roll the pastry into a rough circle (30 cm in diameter) – approximately 4 mm thick. Place on a lightly buttered baking sheet and gently but firmly crimp the edges, over-lapping each little section as your fingers move around the circum-ference. The finished product should look like a circle with a small shallow ridge around the outside. Place in the fridge for up to an hour to chill.

PREHEAT THE OVEN TO 175°C
With a fork prick the surface in a few places, except the ridge.

Bake for 20–25 minutes, or until the pastry is puffed and golden, turning the tray half way through the cooking to make sure the baking is even on each side.

Meanwhile prepare the fruit. Cut the peaches in half and remove the stone. Slice each half into 6 or 8 wedges depending on the size of the fruit. Place in a bowl with the sugar. Jumble together so that the juices start to run a little.

Scatter the fruit evenly over the cooked pastry, leaving the juices in the bowl.

Bake for a further 10 minutes or until the fruits look golden at the edges and the pastry is crisp throughout.

Remove from the oven and slide on to a cooling rack.

TO SERVE
Jumble the raspberries in the peach bowl, coating them in the light sugar syrup, then place them on the peaches decoratively.

Serve warm or cold, dusted with icing sugar, with lots of whipped cream or vanilla ice cream.

SALAD OF DUCK BREAST WITH BALSAMIC–ROASTED PEACHES AND SHALLOTS

4 – 6 duck breasts, depending on size
½ tsp chopped rosemary
1 tsp chopped thyme
1 clove garlic, crushed to a cream
6 tbsp olive oil
3 medium firm but ripe peaches
3 large or 6 small shallots
300 g mixed salad leaves

For the dressing:
2 tbsp balsamic vinegar
5 tbsp olive oil
Salt and pepper
Juice of 1 small orange
2 tsp pomegranate molasses (optional)

With a small sharp knife, remove the skin and fat from each duck breast in one piece. Lay on a baking sheet, cover with cling wrap and freeze, ideally for up to 3 hours or until rigid.

Meanwhile place the duck breasts in a bowl with half the herbs, garlic and olive oil, mix well together and leave at room temperature for a few hours.

PREHEAT THE OVEN TO 175°C

Halve the peaches and remove the stones. Cut each half into equal-sized wedges and lay them in a small baking dish, skin sides down.

Cut the shallots in half lengthwise, peel and carefully remove the root end. Place cut side up in another small baking dish.

Mix the remaining olive oil, crushed garlic and herbs together and drizzle over the two dishes and season each with salt and pepper. (It is best to roast them separately as they have slightly different cooking times.)

Place both dishes in the oven and roast for up to 5–8 minutes, turning occasionally. Divide the balsamic vinegar between them, sprinkling it over evenly, then continue to roast for a few minutes or until the peaches have turned slightly crisp at the edges. Remove them from the oven and allow to cool in their juices while the shallots continue to roast, until they are crisp and golden on the outside and tender on the inside (approximately 5–6 more minutes). Spoon the juices over the shallots to marinate while they cool.

Using a heavy knife, slice the duck fat into thin strips. Place in a heavy-based frying pan and cook over a medium to high heat, stirring occasionally, while the fat is released from the strips and they turn into crisp crackling. Take care as the crackling begins to shrink, as the strips will burn easily. Turn off the heat, remove the crackling with a slotted spoon to a plate lined with kitchen paper. Sprinkle with salt. The resulting duck fat may now be chilled and stored in the fridge or freezer and used for roasting potatoes or root vegetables at a later date.

TURN THE OVEN UP TO 180°C

Without cleaning the pan, sear the duck breasts over a medium to high heat for 2–3 minutes on each side. Remove to an ovenproof dish and roast in the oven for 6–8 minutes. Remove from the oven and cover, then allow the duck to rest for a few minutes while the dish is assembled. Drain all the balsamic juices from the shallots and peaches and mix with any juices which flow from the duck. To this add the remaining dressing ingredients and taste for seasoning.

Place the salad leaves in a bowl and drizzle with a little dressing, toss gently together.

Slice the duck breasts slightly on the angle and place on individual plates attractively. Place the leaves over and around, then tuck the peaches and shallots into the leaves. Scatter with the crackling, then spoon the remaining dressing over and serve immediately.

PURISTS WILL TELL you that for a true Bellini the fresh white peaches (never yellow) should be grated to a pulp (never pureed), before being mixed with chilled Prosecco, the light, fragrant and delicious sparkling wine from the Veneto area of Italy. I personally find grating anything as soft and delicate as a peach not only difficult but also wasteful – the amount of juice one loses! Over hands, around fingers, over the work surface – usually anywhere but in the glass jug.

In fact, I favour all fruit juices to be strained before serving, as I prefer not to have the skin, filaments or 'connective tissue' interfere with the smooth pleasure of a freshly squeezed fruit. We even pass our fresh citrus juices through sieves not once but twice, before serving in the shop or restaurant.

You may not get a job at Harry's Bar in Venice with this recipe and method, but your home will have the chance to become a very popular venue for special summer cocktail parties.

WHITE PEACH BELLINI

4 large ripe white peaches, washed
Caster sugar to taste

Splash of peach liqueur (optional)
1 bottle chilled Prosecco

With a small sharp knife, holding the peaches one by one over a stainless steel pan, cut the flesh away from the stone, allowing the flesh and juices to fall into the pan. Sprinkle over the sugar, cover and place over a medium heat. When the juices come to a simmer, cook for 3–4 minutes or until the peach is very soft and juicy. Pour the entire contents of the pan into a stainless steel sieve and push the contents through with the back of a ladle. Cool over a bowl of iced water. Add the peach liqueur if using, and taste for sweetness.

Pour the peach puree into a glass jug, add a few ice cubes and pour the Prosecco in slowly, as the acidity of the fruit with make the wine foam alarmingly. Stir gently with a long spoon and serve in tall champagne flutes or short shot glasses (as they do in Italy), remembering to pour slowly.

PINE NUT

One fact that I have been most proud of within the restaurant over the past 30 years is that, for the most part, we have made everything ourselves, and used fresh, unprepared ingredients throughout.

Although we buy fresh walnuts, cobnuts and almonds in season, and crack the shells ourselves, I have to say that pine nuts are one of the few exceptions.

I have never tackled a pine cone to extract the nut, and I fear that it would take my staff and me all day, if not all week, to prepare enough to feed our customers for a day.

There seem to be many on the market, at different prices. We buy a beautiful, long and slender pointed pine nut from Spain to serve toasted whole for sprinkling on salads and main courses. The less expensive rounder shaped nuts are perfect for roasting and then chopping or grinding into sauces, oils, macaroons and nut brittle.

A BEAUTIFUL ALTERNATIVE to the classic macaroon, this little sweetmeat is more-ish, crumbly and chewy at the same time. Perfect with a morning coffee, a mug of tea or with an after-dinner espresso.

PINE NUT AND HAZELNUT MACAROONS

35 g hazelnuts
250 g caster sugar
15 g unsalted butter, soft
1 tsp honey

150 g ground almonds
2 egg whites, whisked to a light foam
Approximately 2–3 tbsp pine nuts
Icing sugar for dusting

PREHEAT THE OVEN TO 175°C
Place the hazelnuts on a baking sheet and bake for 10–15 minutes or until they are golden and the skins have begun to peel away. Gently rub them in a tea towel to remove the excess skin, then chop finely by hand or carefully in a food processor.

Mix the sugar, butter and honey together in a small pan and warm briefly over a gentle heat. Add the hazelnuts and almonds. Stir in the egg whites until a soft but not loose mixture is formed.

Chill for a few hours or overnight.

PREHEAT THE OVEN TO 160°C
Line a baking sheet with rice paper or baking parchment. Shape the dough into 18 balls and then roll them one by one in a small bowl filled with the pine nuts until the balls are 'speckled'.

Place on the baking sheet, with plenty of space between them. Bake for approximately 20 minutes or until golden, remove to a cooling rack and store in an airtight container for up to one week. Dust with icing sugar before serving.

Driving through Genoa one summer made me wonder where the fields of basil have gone – it seemed so built up and busy and very much a working sea port. However, I am sure that if I had taken the time to drive into the surrounding hills I would have found the famous basil growing in profusion which I had read so much about in my dog-eared copies of Elizabeth David's books.

Many years ago I stayed in a remote beautiful farmhouse just outside Florence where there was a winter kitchen and a summer kitchen – neither had any electrical equipment. Early each morning I would make the 45 minute drive into the city, to the old market, to buy my ingredients for the day. Rigid and glistening sardines, stunningly beautiful little lettuces from a young brother and sister team who tended their stall each day, green figs, purple figs, both of which were two a penny, white flat-bottomed peaches and of course 20 different varieties of tomato.

One of the first dishes I made in that summer kitchen by hand was a pesto. Traditionally made with a pestle and mortar, I preferred to chop everything by hand as I felt that the brightness of colour would be retained more easily in this way. The pine nuts were toasted with garlic cloves, then chopped together on a dark wooden board. Next the cheese was grated into fine shreds, sea salt and pepper were added, and finally the basil was prepared. The leaves were picked from the stems, laid on top of each other, then with a really sharp knife, chopped quickly and precisely, retaining the fresh brilliantly green hue of the herb.

Dark green local olive oil blended it all into one, the tomatoes were sliced and the sauce dappled over; sardines were on the grill outside and lunch was served.

PESTO

60 g pine nuts, roughly chopped
250 ml olive oil
2 cloves garlic, crushed to a cream
Salt and pepper

1 large bunch basil, approximately 75 g
leaves
75 g grated Parmesan

In a flat heavy-based frying pan heat the pine nuts gently in half the olive oil until golden (about 3–4 minutes). Do not overcook as the taste of the nut will become bitter. Take off the heat and immediately add the garlic cream. Swirl the pan carefully allowing the garlic to blend evenly into the oil. Season with salt and pepper and leave to cool.

Pick the basil leaves from the stems, stack together and chop finely with a sharp knife. Place into a bowl with the remaining olive oil. Pour the pine nuts and flavoured olive oil into the bowl and stir together, then finally fold in the grated Parmesan. Taste and adjust the seasoning.

This may be stored in a screw top jar for up to 10 days, however as with most recipes in this book, the fresher the better.

I AM NOT sure where I found this recipe originally, but it may have been during a journey through the Sicilian hills. I seem to remember visiting a grandmother-, mother- and daughter-run hostelry, a mad crumbling castle of a place, which had rooms as well as dining rooms – some outside and some inside, in elegant but decrepit salons.

Perhaps they had a recipe book to their name or maybe they simply kindly gave it to me. Either way, we have made this torta many times over the years, often serving it with long-poached apricots, plums or peaches in syrup. In the winter it is lovely too, paired with poached dried fruits such as raisins, golden sultanas or prunes.

SICILIAN-STYLE RICOTTA AND PINE NUT TORTA

For the pastry:
180 g flour
Pinch salt
90 g unsalted butter, chilled and diced
60 g caster sugar
2 egg yolks
1 ½ tbsp chilled water

For the ricotta filling:
700 g ricotta
200 g soured cream
65 g caster sugar
Zest of 1 orange
Zest of 1 lemon
75 g candied peel, in small dice
  (page 160)
75 g pine nuts

FOR THE PASTRY

Rub the butter into the flour and salt until it resembles fine bread-crumbs. Stir in the sugar then using a fork, add the yolks and water until amalgamated. Gently knead together until smooth, wrap and chill for up to two hours.

Roll into a disc approximately 25–30 cm across and line a plain or fluted loose bottomed tart tin. Press the pastry gently but firmly into the corners and trim the edges until smooth, and chill for up to an hour. Meanwhile re-roll the trimmings into one long strip, then cut into long ribbons, approximately 1 cm wide, and chill on a baking sheet until required. These will become the latticed top to the torta.

Whip the ricotta and soured cream together until smooth. Add the sugar, citrus zests, candied peel and half the pine nuts.

Pour the mixture into the raw tart, and spread until smooth. Sprinkle with the remaining pine nuts, then using the pastry ribbons, make a lattice criss-cross over the top. Trim the edges and crimp the rim attractively.

PREHEAT THE OVEN TO 175°C

Bake in the centre of the oven for 30 minutes, lower the oven to 160°C and continue to bake for a further 30 minutes or until the filling is set and the pastry is crisp and golden. Cool a little before slicing and serving with poached, pureed or fresh fruits.

POTATO

Potatoes are a wonderful vehicle for pairing with extravagant foods — they have the ability to make the recipient feel a little less ostentatious in eating such luxury.

Baby new season Jersey Royals, served warm and buttered are exquisite draped in crème fraîche and dolloped with caviar. A humble potato salad can be transported to something special with slices of home cured salmon or trout in dill alongside.

More often than not we make gnocchi for our dinner menus each week, with either spinach in the summer or a puree of pumpkin in the autumn. The potatoes are baked in their skins, then scooped out and mixed with nutmeg, sea salt, herbs, egg and a little flour before shaping. The delicious, often misshapen skins which remain are usually fried and served at staff meal time — simply sprinkled with salt, with a dollop of soured cream. It occurred to me one day that perhaps the customers would appreciate these too — and they do! See Fried Potato Skins with White Truffle Mascarpone, page 211.

I NEVER TIRE of sitting in the café at Chez Panisse, looking into the kitchen and especially into the brick-built pizza oven. Their pizza are thin and crisp, cooked in just a few minutes and topped each day with an ever changing selection of ingredients. Nettles with pecorino, or wafer-thin slices of multi-coloured peppers with purple basil, or finely sliced wild mushrooms with buffalo mozzarella.

Perhaps the most surprising menu item I found there in my very early days was a pizza of young potatoes. To my untrained eye this seemed to be an overkill of starches, but I should have had more faith! The little potatoes had been sliced, roasted and then baked on the dough with summer savory (perhaps my favourite herb), and a creamy-stringy cheese, possibly Taleggio. As it emerged from the oven a delicate amount of rocket leaves was strewn over the surface. I have never forgotten it.

POTATO PIZZA WITH TALEGGIO, BASIL AND RED ONION

15 g fresh yeast (or 7 g dry yeast or
   3.5 g easy-blend yeast)
200 ml milk
60 ml olive oil
150 g strong white flour, or '00' flour, or
   half and half
1 tsp salt
500 g very small potatoes

Olive oil
Salt and pepper
2 tsp summer savory or thyme
1 tbsp fine polenta
1 medium red onion, peeled, halved and
   sliced paper-thin
150 g Taleggio, sliced thinly
Basil, rocket leaves, landcress or parsley

If using fresh yeast, whisk into the milk and oil and leave in a warm place until it starts to froth a little. If using dry or easy-blend yeast, simply whisk the milk and oil together.

Mix the flours together with the dry or easy-blend yeast, salt and, either by hand or with the dough hook attachment of a machine, mix the liquids into this until well amalgamated. Continue to knead until a smooth elastic dough is formed. Cover the bowl with clingwrap and leave in a warm place until the dough has almost doubled in size.

PREHEAT THE OVEN TO 180°C

While the dough is proving, wash and slice the potatoes finely, jumble with a drizzle of olive oil, salt and pepper and spread out over an oiled baking sheet. Sprinkle with half the summer savory or thyme and roast until golden, approximately 15–20 minutes.

With a dusting of flour roll the dough into two evenly sized balls, then roll with a rolling pin until thin and approximately round in shape. Lift the discs up one by one and rotate them around in your fingers, allowing the dough to be pulled downwards by gravity. This will make the pizza thinner and more crisp when cooked.

Sprinkle two baking sheets with fine polenta and lay each disc on top carefully. Brush with olive oil then scatter with the sliced raw red onion, the cooked potatoes, the remaining chopped herbs, salt and pepper. Bake for 10–15 minutes or until pale golden. Remove from the oven and place the Taleggio over the top, return to the oven and bake for a further 2–3 minutes or until the cheese has started to melt.

Scatter over a few leaves of basil, rocket, landcress or parsley and serve immediately.

THIS DISH DOES not have to be served with truffles – they are not easy to locate and not easy to afford – but try the dish nonetheless, without. In the absence of the real thing, a small summer truffle which is grey/brown inside and occasionally found in specialist food shops may be used. Alternatively white truffle oil is pungent and will be delicious simply drizzled over the finished dish.

FRIED POTATO SKINS WITH WHITE TRUFFLE MASCARPONE

6 medium potatoes (1.4 kg approximately), Désirée or King Edward, with unblemished skins
Fine salt
250 g mascarpone
Salt and pepper

1 small red onion, finely diced
1 tbsp finely chopped parsley
1 tsp white truffle oil (optional)
Vegetable oil
2 tsp chopped thyme
1 small white or black truffle (optional)

PREHEAT THE OVEN TO 175°C

Scrub and rinse the potatoes, pierce with a few fork marks and place in a flat terracotta dish or on a baking sheet. Sprinkle generously with fine salt. Bake in the oven until tender when pierced with a knife (approximately 45 minutes). When just cool enough to handle (but not cold) cut in half and scoop out the flesh. Use this to make gnocchi or fluffy mashed potatoes.

Cut the skins into even-sized pieces, triangular or wide strips, and leave chilled until ready to serve.

Meanwhile whip the mascarpone with salt, pepper, finely diced red onion, parsley and white truffle oil, if using. Leave covered in the fridge. If a truffle is being used, brush it thoroughly until clean and leave in a cool place, wrapped in soft paper.

One-third fill a heavy-based pan with vegetable or corn oil and heat to or until a small piece of potato skin sizzles and colours within a few seconds. Carefully lower the skins into the fat, a few at a time and fry until crisp and golden. Remove to a bowl lined with several layers of kitchen paper and keep warm until the remaining skins are cooked. Sprinkle with salt, pepper and chopped thyme and serve with the pot of mascarpone on the side.

If extra white truffle oil is available, drizzle a little over the top of the mascarpone. If neither a truffle nor truffle oil is available, simply use extra chopped herbs, such as chives, to scatter or a few dried chilli flakes, and a selection of herb leaves to finish.

Shave the truffle (if using) over the potato skins at the table – it will smell amazing – and eat immediately.

OK – SO WHAT are our collective views on the perfect, roast potato? The outside – crisp, golden, singed edges, shining with traces of fat, speckled with cracked pepper and sea salt perhaps? The interior – searingly hot – fluffy, flaky, slightly sweet, dryish but moist at the same time, slightly salty, with a flavour that says 'this is a real potato – grown by a real person' perhaps?

You may well be a wonderful cook, you may have the most beautiful oven and the best duck fat from last week's roast, but if you do not have the right potatoes you are only going to make mediocre roast potatoes.

In the autumn, winter and early spring months, choose Désirée, Cara, Romano or King Edward – they are the ones which have a floury texture once cooked, as opposed to a firm and waxy interior.

PERFECT ROASTED POTATOES

1.2 kg potatoes	Salt and pepper
150 g duck fat, dripping or 100 ml light	
olive oil and 50 g butter	

Wash the potatoes well and, if the skins are thin, do not peel unless you prefer to. Cut them into even-sized chunks and place in a pan with a generous amount of salt. Cover with cold water and bring swiftly to the boil. Cook for 5–8 minutes or until a knife pierces the outside easily, the inside remaining firm. Drain well and leave covered for a few minutes.

While the potatoes are coming to the boil, preheat the oven to 180°C. Put the duck fat, dripping or olive oil and butter into a terracotta or ovenproof dish, which will hold the potatoes comfortably in one layer, and place it in the oven. When the oven has heated, remove the hot dish and tip the potatoes into the fat carefully (as it may splash and burn you). Shake the dish a little until all the potatoes are level, sprinkle with salt and pepper and roast for up to 30 minutes. Shake the pan again to release the pieces which may have stuck, turning over each piece if necessary, so that they brown evenly. Return the dish to the oven for up to 15 more minutes or until they are crisp, golden, singed at the edges and looking a picture. Remove with a slotted spoon to a warm serving dish and serve as soon as possible.

QUINCE

I have a neighbour who has one quince tree — I do not. As summer turns into autumn, I watch the fruits ripen over the south facing wall, willing them to stay on the branches until I have plucked up the courage to ask her, yet again, if I can collect some of them — if not all! Occasionally I see walkers pass the tree and look quizzically up at the fruit, then attempt to pick one, then waste it. They are often unaware that they are not apples, and furthermore, not edible until prepared and cooked. They require a great deal of time and attention to detail before being ready and fit for purpose.

Each year I long for gifts of quince from various sources and to each friend I give at Christmas a jar or two of quince jelly or quince paste as a thank you. Thank you.

There is an English lady who lives in the San Francisco Bay Area who makes the most delicious and unusual jams, chutneys and relishes out of organic fruits and vegetables. Each Saturday June Taylor stands at her market stall at the Ferry Building, come rain or shine, offering tastings of her products to passers-by. Even though her products are expensive, she sells a lot of pots, so loyal is her following.

Her combinations of flavours are interesting, sometimes quirky, but always delicious. She uses quince often in the autumn and winter months and makes jellies and cheeses out of them, sometimes using plums, apples and herbs also. The Quince and Port Cheese recipe, which we use in our Production Kitchen when quince are plentiful, reminds me of a combination that June might use.

QUINCE AND PORT CHEESE WITH BAY LEAVES

3 kg quince
4 bay leaves
Peelings and juice of 2 large lemons

3.5 kg (approximately) granulated sugar
1½ small glass of ruby port

Wash the quince well, removing the down. Chop the fruit, including peel and core, roughly into walnut-sized pieces and place in a heavy-based stainless steel pan. Barely cover with cold water, add the bay leaves, lemon peelings and juice, cover with a lid and bring slowly to the simmer. Cook for up to an hour or until the fruit, seeds and skin are very soft.

Remove the bay leaves, allow to cool a little and pass the contents of the pan through a wide-gauged sieve or a vegetable mill. Measure the resulting liquid and weigh an equal amount of granulated sugar (eg 1 litre of pulp = 1 kilo sugar). Wash and dry the pan and fill with the liquid and the sugar. Bring slowly to the boil and simmer until the sugar has completely dissolved.

Now comes the dangerous bit. Using rubber gloves, stir the mixture over a medium-high heat, as it thickens. It is important that the base of the pan does not burn the sugar, so constant stirring is vital until the spoon leaves a clear channel on the base of the pan. It will spit and splutter as it thickens, and the stove top will need a spring clean afterwards.

Take the cheese off the heat and stir in the port carefully. Again, it may splutter dangerously.

Line a small plastic tub with two layers of silicone wax paper, pushing it into the corners well and allowing an overhang. Pour the quince into the tub and wrap the excess silicone over neatly. Allow to cool and wrap in clingwrap tightly. Store in a cool dark place for up to eight weeks or in a fridge once the silicone paper has been removed.

Serve with cheeses, radishes and celery heart.

ROASTED QUINCE WITH VANILLA PANNA COTTA

For the fruit:
3 medium even-sized quince
Juice and peelings of 2 lemons
250 ml white wine
½ stick cinnamon, broken
½ vanilla pod, split lengthwise
75 g caster sugar
Peelings of 1 orange

For the panna cotta:
700 ml double cream
½ vanilla pod, split lengthwise
80 g sugar
Peelings of 1 small lemon
3 tsp powdered gelatine

FOR THE FRUIT

Wash the quince and cut into quarters. Peel and core each piece carefully with a small sharp knife. This is not as easy as it sounds – the core is hard and tough; it needs concentration and a steady hand. Make sure that all the core is removed as this will never be rendered tender during cooking.

As each piece is prepared, place it in a bowl with the lemon juice, tossing them gently together occasionally. Place them with the juice in a stainless steel pan, large enough to fit them snugly. Add the wine, cinnamon, vanilla, sugar and citrus peels and just enough water to cover them.

Bring to the boil, cover with a disc of silicone wax paper and push a small lid down inside the pan, on top of the paper, to ensure that the fruits are totally submerged by the juices as they cook. Simmer for 30–40 minutes or until they feel tender when pierced with a skewer. Remove from the heat and allow to cool in the liquid.

TO MAKE THE PANNA COTTA

Heat the cream with the vanilla, sugar and lemon peel for 5–10 minutes over a very low heat. Place the gelatine in a small cup, pour a splash of boiling water over it and stir until it has melted. Add this to the cream and stir until very well blended. Remove the vanilla pod and scrape a little of the seeds into the cream – these little seeds are vital to the look of the panna cotta. Strain the cream into a jug and add 2 or 3 tablespoons of quince syrup to taste. It should not be over-sweet.

Pour into six moulds or little pots. (The panna cotta may be served in the pots or tipped out – although this is more risky.)

Cover with clingwrap and chill for at least an hour or until set – they should have a very slight wobble to them when knocked.

PREHEAT THE OVEN TO 175°C
Remove the fruit from the syrup and slice each piece into 3 or 4 wedges, depending on the size. Lay the slices in a baking dish and cover with a little of the syrup. Bake for 15–20 minutes or until the fruit has deepened in colour and the syrup has almost disappeared. Remove carefully to a plate.

TO SERVE
Either flood the top of each pot with some of the remaining syrup and decorate with the quince slices, or place each pot into a bath of very hot water (a small saucepan is good for this) for a few seconds, or until the panna cotta can be turned upside down onto a plate. The pretty vanilla seeds should be visible at the base of the cream. Decorate with the quince slices and drizzle with a little syrup.

Reserve the leftover syrup for poaching other fruits or for pouring over vanilla ice cream.

Serve with Pistachio Nut Wafers (page 221).

As I HAVE written in my first book, 'there is only one way to make a tarte Tatin – and that is properly'. I still adhere to this – the method is very important, as is the cooking time, and the correct measuring of the butter and sugar.

QUINCE AND ROSEMARY TARTE TATIN

3 medium quince
3 medium apples, ideally medium-sweet and firm, with a low water content, such as Granny Smith, Braeburn or Golden Delicious

150 g soft unsalted butter
125 g caster sugar
1 ½ tsp finely chopped rosemary, plus a few sprigs
400 g puff pastry

Choose a shallow heavy-based frying pan which can go into the oven.

Peel, quarter and core the quince and cut each piece in half lengthwise. Poach the pieces as described in the previous recipe.

Prepare the apples by quartering, peeling and coring.

Spread the butter over the entire base of an 18–20cm shallow frying pan and sprinkle over the sugar evenly. Next, sprinkle the finely chopped rosemary, then alternate the apple quarters and cooked quince wedges, curved sides down on top of the sugar, in a circular fashion until the surface is completely covered. There will be a few apple pieces in excess and these should be placed on top.

Place the pan over a high heat and cook until the butter and sugar start to turn golden, while carefully (as the sugar will be dangerously hot) pushing the excess apple pieces into any gaps which may appear.

While the apples are cooking, roll the pastry to an approximate disc of 20cm across.

PREHEAT THE OVEN TO 170°C
When the fruits have started to turn a dark golden colour on the underside, remove the pan from the heat. Place the pastry on top and push carefully down into the sides. Cut a small slit in the centre as a steam hole.

Bake in the pan, placed on a baking sheet (to catch any caramel drips), for 35–40 minutes or until the pastry is puffed and brown.

Remove from the oven and allow to cool slightly. Place a large plate upside down over the tart and, with a firm hand wrapped in a thick cloth, grasp hold of the pan handle. Place the other hand, also protected by a cloth, on the base of the plate. Pressing the pan and the plate firmly and securely together, tip the pan upside down over the plate, allowing all the juices to arrive on the plate with the tarte.

If necessary, use a small knife to rearrange the fruit pieces, if they have slipped during the 'flight'.

Decorate with rosemary sprigs and serve as soon as possible with crème fraîche or whipped cream.

PISTACHIO NUT WAFERS

60 g egg white (whites from
    approximately 3 eggs)
65 g caster sugar

85 g plain flour
175 g shelled pistachio nuts (not salted)

PREHEAT THE OVEN TO 180°C
Butter and flour a loaf tin, 18 x 8cm.

Whisk the whites and sugar together until a soft peak is formed at the top of the whisk. Mix the flour and nuts together and then gently fold them into the whites carefully but thoroughly. Scoop the mixture into the prepared tin and gently flatten with a wet spatula.

Bake for 25–30 minutes or until golden brown and firm to the touch. Cool, remove from the tin, wrap tightly and ideally leave for 24 hours.

The following day, preheat oven to 160°C. Slice the loaf lengthwise as finely as possible using a serrated knife. Lay the slices, slightly overlapping on a baking sheet and bake for 5–10 minutes or until crisp but not coloured. This makes approximately 30 wafers. Store in an airtight container for up to a week.

RASPBERRY

The wonderful thing about growing raspberries oneself is that the more you pick, the more they produce! Many years ago my brother Tim gave me an *Autumn Bliss* plant which to my amazement and joy, grows back every year, becoming bushier and producing more shoots than the previous year.

Even though I think of raspberries as a summer fruit, the best often arrive from Scotland in the early autumn, and continue right the way into October. In fact, even as I write this, in early November, I am still able to buy delicious, juicy and sweet raspberries for the restaurant menus from British growers.

W E HAVE A little 17th century rented cottage in the country which has a small garden. There are herbs and Jerusalem artichokes, strawberries, wild strawberries and landcress in modest quantities. What I have in large quantities however are apples and Autumn Bliss raspberries. According to the Royal Horticultural Society, the apples are an American variety called Mother – not a great 'eater' but lovely to cook with, for both pies and purees.

At the end of the summer one year I harvested the last remaining apples and raspberries, combining them to make a butter or curd. Without weighing scales (or any clue of where I was heading) I managed to create a lovely soft spread which we later used on toast and muffins, with ice cream and meringues.

APPLE AND RASPBERRY CURD

500 g Bramley or similar sharp apples
150 g unsalted butter
A splash of water

250 g granulated sugar
200 g raspberries
Juice of 1 large lemon

Peel and core the apples and slice thinly. Place in a stainless steel pan with the butter, water and sugar. Place the raspberries on top and cover with a lid. Bring to a gentle simmer, shaking the pan occasionally to prevent sticking. Keep the lid on to retain steam, and cook for up to 10–15 minutes or until the fruits have softened completely.

Preheat the oven to 130°C. Wash three jam jars meticulously, place them on a baking sheet and warm in the oven for 3–5 minutes to sterilise them. Bring the lids to the boil in a small pan of water. Remove the jars carefully with oven gloves and place next to each other on a clean work bench.

Give the apple mixture a whisk and taste, adding either sugar or a little lemon juice.

Carefully fill the jars with the curd to their necks. Lift the lids out of the water one by one and, with a clean tea towel, screw them on tight. Leave them to cool then wash the jars with hot soapy water, polish dry and then store in a dark cool cupboard for up to 2 months.

M Y BROTHERS WENT to a wonderful prep school in Guildford which was especially known for its excellence in music and sport. I well remember at age 10 or 11, attending the summer sports day, for which the Headmaster's wife would prepare an elaborate buffet lunch each year. Her pièce de résistance was her red fruit jelly, which would astound me, even then, by how she managed to hold so much fruit together in so little jelly.

RASPBERRY JELLY

125 g blackcurrants
125 g raspberries
300 g strawberries
60 g sugar

150 ml water
300 ml apple juice
4 tsp powdered gelatine

Pick through the blackcurrants, removing the tails, and check the raspberries for stalks. Hull and slice the strawberries. Place the currants and then the raspberries in a stainless steel pan with the sugar, water and apple juice. Bring to the boil, without stirring, remove from the heat and cover.

Place the gelatine in a small bowl, pour over a little of the warm juices, stir until melted and without a trace of graininess (approximately one minute). Pour the gelatine mixture directly into the fruits and stir very gently so as not to break up the fruit. Place the sliced strawberries into the serving bowl and pour over the fruits and liquid. Give it one final stir, cover and place in the fridge until set. Serve with whipped double cream and Lavender Shortbread (page 227).

THE BEST SMOOTHIES are made with a soft ingedient that acts as a thickener. Bananas are the perfect choice for a luscious brunch or breakfast drink.

Raspberries make the prettiest drinks, but the seeds need to be removed for the perfect texture. As a treat, add a scoop of vanilla ice cream and a few raspberries for decoration.

SMOOTHIE

3 ripe bananas
2 punnets ripe raspberries
250 ml whole milk

250 ml natural yoghurt
A few ice cubes
Cane sugar to taste (optional)

Place the bananas and raspberries into a liquidiser with the milk, yoghurt and ice cubes. Puree until smooth, taste and add a little sugar if required. Pour through a stainless steel sieve into a jug, and using a ladle, press all the juice through. Discard the seeds and serve as soon as possible.

LAVENDER SHORTBREAD

1 tsp finely chopped lavender blossoms
  (approximately 3 heads)
100 g caster sugar, plus a little extra for
  finishing

200 g unsalted butter, soft
300 g plain flour
A pinch of salt

PREHEAT THE OVEN TO 160°C

Mix the lavender with the sugar and cream into the butter until light. Sieve the flour and salt together and mix into the butter to make a soft dough. Wrap and chill for at least and hour.

Roll the dough to approximately 5mm thick and cut into discs with a 3–4cm fluted cutter. Lay on a baking sheet lined with silicone paper. Sprinkle with a little sugar and bake for 15–20 minutes or until pale golden. The shortbread will become crisp on cooling. Store in an airtight container for up to a week. This makes 18–20 biscuits.

ROCKET

Although its use dates back to Roman times, I wonder if there is any other salad leaf which has risen to such prominence or with quite such alarming speed over the past few decades as rocket.

Almost every supermarket carries it now and I would suggest that certainly most of the cafés and restaurants in the land feature it on their menus in some shape or form throughout the year.

Once thought of as simply a weed and part of the mesclun salad selection in the spring and summer months, this leaf, both the wild and the broad-leaf varieties, can offer a wonderful pepperiness to a salad when mixed with a selection of other, less powerful leaves. When really fresh, the leaves are firm and will hold their shape, as well as the other leaves tossed with them, so they are an ideal vehicle to give height to a salad plate and therefore add to the eye appeal of a dish.

Rocket tossed with a little olive oil, salt and lemon juice and scattered over grilled steaks or baked fillets of fish, will add a vibrancy in colour and taste. Or chopped roughly and tossed into pasta or risotto, just before serving, it will add an extra dimension to the flavours.

ONE OF THE joys of owning a restaurant is that usually there is an electric ham slicing machine at hand. We use ours for slicing fennel hearts paper thin for salads, or for day-old bread to bake as wafer toasts for cheeses or dips, or for the artisan-cured meats which we buy from northern Italy and the Pyrenees. In addition, leftover roasted meats may be sliced the following day, much more finely by machine than any expert carver could – and this recipe cries out for one. If I need anything expertly sliced for home, I ask the restaurant to do it for me!

In the absence of a slicing machine, however, use a very sharp long medium-heavy knife, and make sure that all the excess fat and sinew have first been removed and that it is sliced across the grain, not along the grain, in order for it to be served meltingly tender.

A leftover joint of sirloin is probably the best cut of beef to use for this: full of flavour and beautifully tender when rare or medium-rare.

ROCKET WRAPPED IN RARE– ROASTED BEEF, WITH MUSTARD MAYONNAISE ON TOAST

1 *small baguette*
1 *clove garlic, crushed*
2 *tbsp olive oil*
Small handful wild or garden rocket
Approximately 400 g rare-roasted beef
1 *tbsp Dijon mustard*

1 *quantity mayonnaise (page 32)*
Salt and pepper
Olive oil to drizzle
1 *lemon, cut into wedges*
1 *small piece horseradish root*

PREHEAT THE OVEN TO 175°C

Slice the baguette thinly on an angle into 12–18 slices and lay the slices overlapping on a baking sheet. Mix the crushed garlic with olive oil and drizzle over the bread as evenly as possible. Bake for 5–10 minutes or until golden. Leave to cool.

Wash and spin the rocket leaves, removing any thick stems or discoloured leaves.

Trim most of the excess fat from the beef and lay it flat side down on a chopping board. Holding it firmly with one hand, slice the meat

— 231 —

into 12–18 cardboard-thin slices and lay them slightly overlapping on a tray. Cover and keep cool until ready to assemble.

Mix the mustard with the mayonnaise, taste and adjust seasoning.

One by one, using approximately a third of the mayonnaise, dollop a small teaspoonful of mayonnaise on to each toast and lay decoratively on a serving platter.

Place the slices of beef one by one on a chopping board, cover with a few leaves of rocket, then small dollops of the remaining mayonnaise. Roll the 'parcel' up, allowing a few leaves to show at each end. Place each one on a toast, firmly sticking it on to the mayonnaise. To serve, drizzle with a little olive oil, grate over the horseradish, and offer lemon wedges.

THE RIVER CAFE in London has been one of my favourite watering- and sustenance-holes for over two decades. I find their taste and style inviting, exciting and delicious. In the winter I often choose their bollito misto – usually made with veal shin, cotechino, ox tongue and sometimes capon, which they serve sliced, with poached vegetables, together with a light but robust-tasting broth and horseradish. They often serve a second accompaniment with it, a version of salsa verde: chopped green herbs with capers, mustard, sea salt and shallot, but for this dish they add roughly chopped hard-boiled egg.

This recipe is an adaptation of this idea and uses rocket leaves as the main herb. It may be used as a sauce to accompany grilled or poached meats, fish, soft cheeses such as mozzarella or fresh goat cheese, or as a dip with crudités or little toasts.

ROCKET SALSA VERDE WITH CAPERS AND CHOPPED EGG

3 large eggs
Handful of rocket leaves, chopped
   medium-fine
2 tbsp medium-finely chopped parsley
1 tbsp medium-finely chopped mint
½ tbsp medium-finely chopped
   marjoram
1 tbsp finely snipped chives

120 ml olive oil
Salt
2 small shallots or 1 small onion
1 tbsp baby capers, drained from brine or
   rinsed of salt
Zest of 1 lemon
1 small chilli, finely chopped (optional)

Cook the eggs in boiling water for 7 minutes, rinse under ice cold water and peel. Detach the white from the yolk. Crumble or sieve the yolk and roughly chop the white. Leave to one side.

Mix the chopped rocket, parsley, mint, marjoram and chives together with the olive oil and salt. Finely dice the shallot or onion and add together with the capers, lemon zest and chilli, if using. Taste for seasoning – it should be piquant and salty. Finally fold the egg in gently and serve within 24 hours.

ROCKET AND POTATO FRITTATA

3 tbsp olive oil
700 g cooked potato, cut into small
   cubes
½ bunch spring onions, washed and
   trimmed
9 eggs
Salt and pepper
1 ½ tbsp finely chopped chives

6 tbsp milk
80 g rocket leaves, washed and spun dry

To serve:
150 ml crème fraîche
Your choice of smoked salmon, crisp
   pancetta, soft goat cheese

This is a quick and easy supper or brunch dish – all you need is very fresh eggs, a perfect non-stick pan and some eager appetites at the table.

Heat the overhead grill in the oven.

Slice the spring onion finely. Warm the olive oil in the pan until hot, add the cubes of potato and fry until they are golden, stirring occasionally. Add the spring onions. Whisk the eggs together with the salt, pepper, chives and milk, until frothy.

Pour the eggs into the pan and shake to disperse the potato evenly. Leave over a high heat while the eggs start to cook around the edges. Scatter the rocket leaves over the top and using a wooden spoon, press them gently into the frittata.

Immediately place the pan under the grill and cook for a few minutes, or until it has puffed and become set to your liking (it should be slightly runny in the centre).

Slide it carefully on to a warm serving dish and serve with crème fraîche, smoked salmon, crumbled crisp pancetta or dollops of fresh goat cheese – or all three.

SAGE

There are many varieties of sage — grey-green leaves, purple-grey leaves, yellow variegated leaves and many more. When not in the herb garden, they are often found in herbaceous borders amongst the lavender and roses. They are hardy plants and come back each year without much tending or persuasion.

An infusion of fresh sage leaves in hot water makes a lovely soothing tisane, to help ward off a sore throat or chesty cold.

I tend to think of sage as a winter herb, as it is heady and heavy in flavour, and matches well the more robust foods, such as onions, garlic, pork, game, guinea fowl and some of the more flavourful fish.

However, it is unpleasant to eat raw, so it is best to either shred or chop the leaves before cooking, to soften them, and to also soften the distinctively full flavour.

O UR SAUSAGE ROLLS are legendary, I believe, and customers travel from far to collect them from the shop. Is it the flaky all-butter puff pastry which we make day in, day out? Or is it the Gloucester Old Spot pork from Plantation Pigs in Surrey which we use, minced not too coarse, not too fine? Or is it the slow cooking of the diced onion with freshly cracked pepper and sea salt – or is it the generous handfuls of freshly chopped soft sage leaves which are folded in to the meltingly delicious onion as it comes off the heat?

This adaptation of the sausage roll is perhaps more akin to a pork pie, whilst retaining the elements of our original.

Here we use a slightly less rich pastry, a short crust top and bottom – which holds the weight of the meat more robustly and makes it a more substantial dish.

PORK, ONION AND SAGE PIE

For the pastry:
400 g plain flour
½ tsp fine salt
200 g chilled butter
2 eggs
Approximately 30 ml chilled water

For the filling:
1 medium onion, peeled and cut into
   small dice
2 tbsp olive oil
Salt and pepper
2 tbsp chopped sage
750 g minced pork
Finely grated zest of 1 lemon
1 egg, whisked with salt to use as egg
   wash

FOR THE PASTRY
Sieve the flour into a bowl with the salt, rub in the butter until the mixture resembles fine breadcrumbs. Alternatively, mix together in a mixing machine on a low speed, using the paddle. A food processor could be used, with the pulse action, but care should be taken once the butter is added as it could overmix if left too long. Add the eggs one by one, bringing the dough together. Add a little water if needed. Knead gently to form a smooth ball, wrap and chill for up to an hour.

Roll the pastry into two discs – approximately 30 cm in diameter, one slightly smaller than the other. Line a loose-based tart tin, approximately 26 cm in diameter, with the larger disc, pressing it carefully into the corners. Chill in the fridge for a minimum of 30 minutes. Chill the second disc on a plate at the same time.

PREHEAT THE OVEN TO 180°C
Place a sheet of baking parchment into the lined tart, fill this with baking beans and bake for 20–25 minutes. Carefully remove the paper and baking beans and return the tart to the oven for a further 5 minutes to cook until the base is pale golden in colour.

FOR THE FILLING
Meanwhile cook the onion over a medium heat with olive oil, salt and pepper, stirring constantly so that it does not colour. When soft, add almost all the chopped sage and remove from the heat. Allow to cool.

Place the minced pork in a large bowl and mix in the onion and lemon zest either by hand or with a robust spoon, until thoroughly amalgamated. Fry a small piece in a pan to test the seasoning and adjust if necessary.

Press the pork mixture gently but firmly into the tart shell, giving the centre a slight domed shape. Brush the rim of the tart with the egg wash then cover with the chilled second pastry disc, pressing down firmly, especially at the edges where the cooked and uncooked pastries join. Crimp the edges decoratively.

Brush the top with the remaining egg wash, sprinkle with a little salt and the remaining chopped sage and cut a small cross in the centre to act as a steam-hole.

Turn the oven up to 200°C and bake for up to 15 minutes, then turn the temperature down to 180°C and bake for a further 20–25 minutes or until a metal skewer feels piping hot when removed from the centre.

Remove from the oven, and serve either immediately, or cool and serve with salad leaves with mustard dressing, radishes and gherkins.

SWEET POTATO MASH WITH CRISP SAGE LEAVES, RICOTTA AND PECAN NUTS

1.5 kg sweet potatoes
2 tsp cumin seeds
2 tbsp light olive oil
100 g butter, plus a little extra for
   buttering dish
1 bunch sage, small leaves picked, large
   leaves chopped finely

1 small red chilli, finely chopped
2 cloves garlic, crushed to a cream
Salt
50 g pecans, medium-finely chopped
250 g ricotta or fresh goat cheese

Peel the sweet potatoes and place in a large pan of boiling salted water, cover and simmer until tender to the centre. Drain in a colander and when cool enough to handle, cut roughly into smallish pieces.

Toast the cumin seeds in a small pan over a medium heat until they are fragrant – do not allow to burn. Crush using a pestle and mortar, or in a spice grinder.

Meanwhile heat the olive oil and half the butter in a pan until foaming. Fry the small sage leaves until crisp (though not too dark), remove with a slotted spoon and drain on kitchen paper. Add the remaining butter to the pan and add the ground cumin, chopped chilli and chopped sage and cook until fragrant (approximately one minute). Remove from the heat, add the garlic and stir well.

Place the sweet potato in a large bowl and beat with a hand whisk or electric whisk until smooth. Little by little add almost all the seasoned butter ingredients until well amalgamated. Add salt to taste.

PREHEAT THE OVEN TO 175°C

Brush an ovenproof dish with butter and spoon the potato mash in, levelling the top a little. Drizzle over any remaining melted butter and bake for 8–10 minutes.

Remove from the oven and scatter the pecans with crumbled ricotta or goat cheese on the top, and continue to bake for a further 3–4 minutes or until piping hot.

Garnish with the fried sage leaves and serve alongside a crisp green and bitter leaf salad, or with roasted pork, turkey or chicken.

SAGE AND ANCHOVY SANDWICH FRITTERS

24 sage leaves
6 whole anchovies or 12 fillets
1 large egg
Salt and pepper
100 g dried breadcrumbs (page 139)

Vegetable oil
Fine salt
1 handful parsley leaves, washed and
    thoroughly dried
A few lemon wedges

Pick the large sage leaves from a bunch (approximately 20–24 evenly sized leaves) and lay half of them like soldiers on a board. In a bowl of cold water rinse the anchovies, remove the fillets from each fish and drain on kitchen paper. Alternatively drain 12 fillets from a can of prepared anchovies. Place one fillet on each leaf, then the remaining sage leaves on top, to make a sandwich. Press together and skewer each with a toothpick along the length.

Whisk the egg with salt and pepper in a small bowl and place the dried breadcrumbs in another bowl. Using one hand for wet and one hand for dry, dip the sage sandwiches, one by one, into the egg to coat them. Lift out, allowing any excess egg to drain back into the bowl. Immediately dip them into the crumbs, shaking the bowl to coat them all over and then place them on a plate until ready to fry. Preheat the oven to 150°C.

Fill a large heavy-based pan one-third full with vegetable oil and heat to approximately 170°C or until a breadcrumb sizzles immediately on entering the oil. Line a baking sheet with copious sheets of kitchen paper. Carefully remove the toothpicks, press the sandwiches firmly together and fry a few at a time until crisp and golden. They will fry in 4–5 seconds. Remove with a slotted spoon to the kitchen paper, sprinkle with fine salt (yes even anchovies need a little salt!) and place in a cool oven while the remainder are fried. Finally fry the dry parsley leaves – with great care as they will splutter when they hit the oil (so have a lid nearby).

Serve the fritters as soon as possible with wedges of lemon and sprinkled with the fried parsley.

SQUASH AND PUMPKIN

Tessa Traeger grew all these pumpkin and squash in her garden in North Devon and then photographed them, before bringing them to London to enjoy.

I have had limited success with squash in my garden, even though it seems that the pumpkin family has a way of growing well in most types of soil and in most types of weather conditions.

There is something rather special about the sight of a market stall laid out in the height of autumn. The colours and shapes of the squash on view are tantalising, and tempt the keen cook to experiment with a variety of dishes. From soups and stews to roasts, or sliced and grilled or baked and partnered with garlic and cream or tomato and herbs, the opportunities to create interesting and nourishing dishes are endless.

In my first book I wrote a recipe for a pumpkin soup which is made with, and served from, the pumpkin itself. The 'lid' of the pumpkin is first removed and the seeds scooped out. A garlic and herb-infused cream is then poured into the cavity and the whole thing is baked in the oven until tender. Scooped out into warm soup bowls and served with a warm crusty baguette, it is the ideal dish to serve as the cooler evenings draw in.

I N MOST LATE autumn vegetable patches there will be one courgette that has been forgotten and allowed to grow into the size of
a marrow. The following recipe is perfect for this.

BAKED MARROW WITH SAGE CRUMBS

1.5 kg marrow
6 thick slices day-old bread, crusts
   removed
2 cloves garlic, crushed to a cream
80 ml olive oil

Salt and pepper
1 tbsp chopped sage
150 g ricotta salata, pecorino or other
   crumbly cheese

Wash the marrow and cut in half lengthwise and then in half across.
Remove any large or hard seeds with a spoon.

Using a food processor, grind the bread until it resembles rough
crumbs.

Place the marrow pieces into a pan of boiling salted water and cook
for one or two minutes or until the flesh just starts to become tender.

Drain and when cool enough to handle, place the cut surfaces on a
chopping board and slice across in thin slices, keeping the marrow
together.

Choose an oven-to-table baking dish large enough to contain all the
marrow. Mix the garlic with the olive oil and drizzle half into the dish
and season with salt and pepper.

Gently fan the marrow quarters on the board, skin sides up, and
lift them carefully one by one into the dish, fitting them neatly and
snugly together.

PREHEAT THE OVEN TO 175°C
Sprinkle the marrow with the sage, breadcrumbs, salt and pepper and
drizzle with the remaining olive oil. Bake for 15−20 minutes or until
the marrow is tender and the crumbs crisp and golden.

If the crumbs start to colour too soon, cover with a piece of foil and
continue to bake until ready.

While still hot, scatter with the crumbled cheese and as it begins to
melt, serve with a salad of bitter leaves or tomatoes.

Although this is a rustic dish, and should therefore look a little 'homely' when presented, it is advisable to take care when slicing the vegetables, so that the individual ingredients look uniform in shape and size.

SPICED PUMPKIN, TOMATO AND CHICKPEA STEW

2 kg pumpkin or squash, blue hubbard, crown prince, onion squash or similar
1 tsp cumin seeds
1 tsp coriander seeds
½ tsp yellow or black mustard seeds
4 cardamom pods
100 ml vegetable or light olive oil
2 cloves garlic crushed to a cream
1 small green or red chilli, finely chopped (with seeds if extra heat is preferred)
1 large onion, peeled and finely sliced
2 sticks celery, finely sliced on the angle
1 fennel bulb, finely sliced
1 tsp salt
1 litre vegetable or chicken stock
½ bunch coriander, washed, leaves kept whole and stalks finely chopped
4 large tomatoes
350 g cooked chickpeas (canned are fine)
Large handful of flat-leaf parsley, roughly chopped

Wash the pumpkin or squash and cut into large wedges. Remove the tough outer skin and the hard seeds. Cut into pieces the size of a walnut.

In a small pan gently heat all the spices together for a few minutes or until they are fragrant. Do not allow them to burn. Remove the husks of the cardamom and add the seeds to the remaining spices. Crush them together in a pestle and mortar or grind in a spice grinder.

Heat the oil and spices together in a large, heavy-based pan with the garlic and chilli, over a medium heat, stirring continuously to avoid burning.

When the oil starts to become aromatic (approximately 1–2 minutes), add the pumpkin, onion, celery and fennel, stir well, coating everything in the infused oil. Add salt and cook together for a few minutes until the vegetables begin to soften. Add the stock and the chopped coriander stalks and cover with a lid. Simmer for up to 20 minutes or until the vegetables have become tender throughout.

Meanwhile blanch the tomatoes for a few seconds in a pan of boiling water. Remove to a bowl of iced water, then peel.

Roughly chop the tomatoes and add to the stew with the chickpeas and continue to simmer for a further 5–10 minutes.

Taste for seasoning and add the parsley and coriander leaves before serving alongside steamed rice, crushed potatoes, baked polenta or just by itself as a robust soup.

ONE OF THE images I look forward to, year on year in the late summer sunshine of the Luberon, is that of the iron bark pumpkins laid out in fields by the roadsides. They are so recognisable, with deep ridges cut into their sides, the shiny skin glinting in the sunshine. I know that within a few weeks they will be loaded onto tractors and some will be boxed up for transport to the London markets.

At the Bakery and Production Kitchen we use them for pumpkin bread, muffins, savoury tarts and soups and in the restaurant we slice and roast or stew them to serve with corn-fed chicken, guinea fowl, pigeon and duck, or with pork and venison dishes.

This focaccia could be served as an accompaniment to soups or salads, but would be perfect simply served with a large chunk of delicious cheese and a slice of Quince and Port Cheese (page 217) for a quick lunch dish. It also makes a great sandwich, split in two and filled with buffalo mozzarella, slices of tomatoes, whole basil leaves and garden rocket. It lasts well for a day or two if wrapped in cling-wrap, and is perfect sliced, drizzled with olive oil and lightly grilled or toasted.

IRON BARK PUMPKIN, ROSEMARY AND PUMPKIN SEED FOCACCIA

250 g iron bark or similar pumpkin or squash, washed, skin removed
Olive oil
Salt and pepper
1 clove garlic, crushed to a cream
2 tsp chopped rosemary, plus a few sprigs

15 g fresh yeast (or 7 g dry yeast or 3.5 g easy-blend)
280 ml warm water
125 ml light olive oil
600 g strong white flour
25 g salt
1 tbsp pumpkin seeds
Salt

PREHEAT THE OVEN TO 170°C
Cut the pumpkin into even-sized slices, approximately 1 cm thick. Place into a bowl with a little olive oil, salt, pepper, garlic and half the chopped rosemary and jumble together until well coated. Lay the pieces on a parchment paper-lined baking sheet and roast in the oven

for 15–20 minutes or until tender and beginning to brown at the edges. Cool, then cut the pumpkin into thumbnail-size dice and retain a few good-looking pieces for the topping of the focaccia.

TO MAKE THE DOUGH

If using fresh yeast, whisk into the water and olive oil and leave in a warm place until it starts to froth a little. If using dry yeast or easy-blend yeast, simply whisk the water and oil together.

Mix the flour (and the dry or easy-blend yeast if using) together with the salt and remaining chopped rosemary and, either by hand or with the dough hook attachment of a machine, mix in the liquids until well amalgamated. Continue to knead until a smooth elastic dough is formed. Cover the bowl with cling wrap and leave in a warm place until the dough has almost doubled in size.

Knead the diced pumpkin and pumpkin seeds into the dough briefly, using a dusting of flour, and then shape into a flat disc approximately 1.5 cm thick.

Well oil a baking sheet and place the focaccia on top, drizzle with olive oil and cover with clingwrap and leave to prove again in a warm place until it has almost doubled its size (approximately 30–40 minutes).

PREHEAT THE OVEN TO 210°C

Remove the clingwrap, gently press the reserved pumpkin pieces and rosemary sprigs into the surface, and using your fingertips, make a few dimple marks over the surface. Sprinkle with a little salt and bake for 12–15 minutes or until risen and golden.

Remove from the oven, drizzle with a little olive oil and serve.

STRAWBERRY

Strawberries seem to arrive earlier and earlier in the markets now — the best traditionally in time for June picnics and festivals, but now, even by April, there are more than acceptable varieties to find.

In March, the San Francisco sun-kissed markets will offer strawberries that not only please the eye, but are also so scented that you will be drawn to the right stall.

I could probably have filled this book with strawberry-related dishes as they are such multi-taskers. Try simmering them with halved, slightly over-ripe purple figs, with half their combined weight in granulated sugar and a splash of lemon juice, to make a pleasing soft-set jam for breakfast.

Or prepare for Christmas and New Year's Eve by making a Rumtopf, the German-style macerated fruit compote, by layering strawberries and other soft fruits with sugar and rum and then leaving them in a glass jar with a lid for six months to mature. With this you could delight friends and family with the surprise of 'fresh' summer fruits, steeped in alcohol, to warm them as they sit by a log fire after walks in the snow.

Or serve simply, as we do at the restaurant in the summer months, just by themselves, with little bowls of crème fraîche and brown sugar, for guests to dip into and eat one by one.

I N   M Y   F I R S T   book I described a meal which I ate in Alain
Ducasse's restaurant in Monaco, one spring day many years ago. It
was completely vegetarian and was composed of the most wonderful salads, herbs, vegetables and fruits of the region. It was sublime.
One of the desserts was both warm and chilled – a little silver bowl
filled with wild strawberries which had been flashed over a scant
amount of heat, perhaps with a tiny amount of vanilla syrup. Then at
the table, the waiter added a scoop of refreshing iced fromage frais
sorbet. Heaven.

The most tricky part of this recipe is the timing. There is nothing
worse, either to eat or to look at, than overcooked strawberries. In fact
they should not cook at all – rather, the warm syrup should be poured
over at the last second, almost as the dessert is about to be eaten.

WARM STRAWBERRIES WITH SORBET OF FROMAGE FRAIS

For the sorbet:	For the strawberries:
150 g caster sugar	*2 large punnets strawberries*
150 ml water	*75 g sugar*
½ vanilla pod, split lengthwise	*150 ml white wine or Prosecco*
300 g fromage frais	

FOR THE SORBET

Bring the sugar, water and vanilla to a rolling boil, simmer for 5 minutes, then scrape the seeds from the pod into the syrup and leave to
cool. The remaining pod may be rinsed and used for another recipe.

Whisk the fromage frais until smooth and stir in the syrup to taste.

Churn in an ice cream machine, following the manufacturer's instructions. Remove from the machine just as it becomes firm, cover
and place in the freezer. This may be stored for up to two weeks but is
best eaten within 24 hours.

FOR THE STRAWBERRIES

Separate the strawberries, roughly half and half – the bruised or over
ripe ones and the perfect, even sized ones. Hull and slice the softer
strawberries into a stainless steel pan, add the sugar, white wine or

Prosecco, cover and simmer for no more than 7–10 minutes or until the syrup is bright red and the strawberries have become pale and wan. Strain the juice through a stainless steel sieve into a clean pan but do not push the debris. The juice should be the colour of a gleaming ruby. Discard the strawberry pulp.

Slice the perfect strawberries into six pretty dessert dishes – glass is best. This may be done a little in advance.

To serve, scoop the sorbet on to the strawberries, whilst bringing the syrup quickly to the boil. Pour into a heat-proof serving jug and serve the dishes at the table, pouring the syrup over and around the strawberries (not the sorbet). Eat while still warm.

SALAD OF STRAWBERRIES WITH SOFT GOAT CHEESE, OLIVES AND PISTACHIO NUTS

1 large punnet strawberries
Salt and pepper
1 tbsp balsamic vinegar
4 tbsp olive oil, plus a little for tossing the salad

2 bunches watercress
1 celery heart
2 tbsp Niçoise olives
1 tbsp pistachio nuts
300 g goat cheese

Remove a few of the softest strawberries from the punnet and chop finely. Place in a bowl with salt, pepper, balsamic vinegar and the olive oil, taste and leave to marinate.

Pick through the watercress, removing large stalks and discoloured leaves, wash and spin gently to dry. Choose the centre leaves and tender stalks of the celery and cut into even-sized pieces.

Slice the remaining strawberries, halve the olives (discarding the stone) and roughly slice the pistachio nuts.

Place the watercress, celery and pistachio nuts in a bowl, drizzle with a little olive oil, salt and pepper and lightly jumble together. Arrange the salad on a serving dish, scatter with the strawberries and olives and then the crumbled goat cheese. Dollop the dressing over and around or serve it separately.

THIS SICILIAN SWEETMEAT street-food treat is a favourite of mine – a perfect sweet snack for any time of day. The fried sweet pasta dough is shaped like a short tube and is traditionally filled with whipped ricotta and candied peel. Nowadays they can be found in many parts of Italy of course, with a variety of fillings. Sadly most are aimed at the mass-market, and for me, lacking in taste or style, as I often find them too full, too sweet and too gaudy.

Whilst the classic cannoli can be eaten walking along a street, at the restaurant, I prefer to serve them slightly lighter in style and deconstructed, allowing the customer to make their own 'cannoli'. The serving platter should be placed in the centre of the table. Each guest should have a few strawberries on their plate, alongside a dollop of the whipped ricotta. They should help themselves to a few fried 'cannoli' at a time and place them onto their plate. Holding one at a time and using a small knife or spoon the ricotta may be spread or scooped onto one end of the 'cannoli'. They should then place a few strawberry slices on top. As the little pastries are so delicate they should be placed in the mouth with great care. Beware, they are rather more-ish!

STRAWBERRY 'CANNOLI'

For the pastry:
80 g caster sugar
3 egg yolks
1 tbsp sunflower or olive oil
1 tbsp grappa or rum
300 g plain or 'oo' flour
½ tsp baking powder
Pinch salt
Vegetable oil for frying
1 tbsp icing sugar mixed with ¼ tsp
  cinnamon, for dusting

For the whipped ricotta:
250 g ricotta
300 ml double cream
1–2 tsp icing sugar
2 tsp candied peel, finely chopped
  (optional, page 160)

Mint leaves, for decoration
2 large punnets strawberries

FOR THE PASTRY
Whisk the sugar and yolks together until pale. Add the oil and grappa and whisk until smooth. Stir the flour, baking powder and salt and

knead until a smooth ball is formed. Wrap well with clingwrap and leave in a cool place for up to an hour.

Divide into 5 or 6 pieces, dust with flour, and roll each into thin strips, either through a pasta machine or a with a rolling pin. Lay each strip onto a chopping board and then cut each into rough triangles. One-third fill a wide heavy-based pan with vegetable oil and heat to 180°c. Test a small piece of dough and if it turns golden within 30 seconds the oil is ready. Fry the 'cannoli' in small batches, gently stirring them in the oil, for even cooking.

Remove the triangles with a slotted spoon to a tray lined with three layers of kitchen paper and sprinkle with a little cinnamon sugar as they cool down.

FOR THE WHIPPED RICOTTA

Place the ricotta in a bowl and whisk a little. It will not become completely smooth, but gently fold in the cream, add a little sugar to taste and the candied peel, if using. Keep chilled until ready to serve.

Pile the fried 'cannoli' on the serving platter and dust the entire plate with the remaining cinnamon sugar. Hull the strawberries and cut in half. Divide the strawberries between the plates and place a scoop of ricotta to the side. Decorate with mint or other pretty leaves and, using a small sieve, dust the entire plate with icing sugar.

SWEETCORN

If I had to live on just a few ingredients, sweetcorn would probably be one of them. Vastly versatile and delicious in so many ways, it lights up my day when the first sweet ears of corn arrive in late summer. I have to say, however, that California can boast about having the best in the world. I believe that I have seen the sweetest little pearls of corn kernels in the San Francisco farmers' market, on the tables of some of the best Bay Area restaurants, and of course within the walls of Chez Panisse. The kernels are almost milk-white and the size of baby's teeth. Sweet and succulent, they are a 'cook-in-two-seconds' kind of corn – a dream.

SWEETCORN BLINIS WITH CORIANDER AND SMOKED SALMON

25 g cornmeal
150 g flour
½ tsp salt
1 tsp baking powder
180 ml warm milk
75 g melted butter, cooled
2 eggs, separated
2 medium sweetcorn
Juice of 1 lime
½ small red chilli, chopped

1 tbsp chopped coriander
50 g butter
2 tbsp olive oil

To serve:
12 slices of smoked salmon
A few pea leaves and coriander sprigs
2 limes, cut into wedges
Crème fraîche or soured cream

Mix the cornmeal, flour, salt and baking powder together. Mix the warm milk and melted butter together and slowly beat in the egg yolks until smooth. Stir the egg mixture into the dry ingredients to make a smooth batter.

To prepare the corn, remove husk and hairs and lay flat on a chopping board. Remove the kernels by running a sharp knife along the length, and place them in a bowl. With the back of the knife carefully scrape the 'milk' from the remaining corn and add to the kernels. Cook the corn in a small amount of boiling salted water, covered, for 3–4 minutes, drain and cool. Add the corn to the batter with the lime juice and chilli. Leave for up to three hours before adding the coriander.

Whisk the egg whites until stiff and gently fold into the batter until blended. Melt the butter and olive oil in a heavy-based frying pan until foaming. Add 3 or 4 tablespoon-sized dollops of the batter at a time to the pan. When each blini is crisp and firm on the base, flip over carefully with a spatula and fry on the other side. This will make a total of 12–14 small blinis. Remove to a tray lined with kitchen paper, and keep warm whilst the remainder are cooked.

TO SERVE
Serve two blinis on each plate. Twist slices of smoked salmon over them then garnish with pea leaves and coriander sprigs. Add lime wedges and dollops of crème fraîche or soured cream, and serve.

BAKED SWEETCORN AND POLENTA PUDDING WITH RICOTTA

750 ml milk
4 bay leaves
A few thyme stalks
2 cloves garlic, crushed
Salt and pepper
100 g polenta or cornmeal, plus extra
   for the dish
100 g grated Parmesan, plus some for
   serving (optional)

3 sweetcorn
250 g ricotta
3 eggs
2 tsp summer savory or thyme
1 clove garlic, peeled and halved
Olive oil

Prepare the corn and cook in a little water as before (page 267).

Rub the base of a terracotta or other ovenproof dish with the halved garlic clove and drizzle with a little olive oil. Sprinkle with a little polenta and a little of the Parmesan.

Heat the milk very gently with the bay leaves, thyme stalks, garlic, salt and pepper for 5–10 minutes. Leave covered, off the heat, to infuse, then strain into a clean pan.

Meanwhile whisk the ricotta with the eggs until smooth, add salt and pepper, half the chopped summer savory or thyme, and the sweetcorn. Taste for seasoning.

Bring the infused milk to the boil and whisk in the polenta, in a steady slow stream, until smooth. Reduce the heat and continue to cook gently, stirring with a wooden spoon for 5–8 minutes or until thick enough to hold its shape on the spoon. Stir in half the remaining Parmesan, taste and pour into a large bowl to cool a little.

PREHEAT THE OVEN TO 170°C
Fold the ricotta mixture into the polenta until well blended. Taste again and then pour the batter into the dish and sprinkle with remaining herbs and the remaining Parmesan.

Bake for 20–25 minutes or until set around the edge and slightly wobbly in the centre.

Serve immediately, with a scattering of extra freshly grated Parmesan over the top if desired.

THIS IS A great way to use a large three-quarters-eaten roast chicken, or two small, with some meat remaining on the bone. If the carcass has very little meat remaining, you may like to use two roast chicken breasts or four cooked boned chicken legs instead.

CHICKEN AND SWEETCORN SOUP

For the broth:
Large roast chicken carcass (see above)
1 small onion, peeled and quartered
1 small carrot, peeled and quartered
2 sticks celery, roughly chopped
2 outside leaves fennel, roughly chopped
4 bay leaves
A few thyme sprigs
A few black peppercorns
1.5 litres water

For the soup:
2 large or 3 small sweetcorn
75 g butter
2 bay leaves
30 g plain flour
300 g potatoes, peeled and cut into small cubes
150 ml double cream
Salt and pepper
1 tbsp roughly chopped flat-leaf parsley

TO MAKE THE BROTH

Remove the useable cooked chicken pieces from the carcass and reserve. Pull or chop the carcass into pieces and place in a heavy-based pan with the vegetables, herbs and peppercorns.

Add cold water to cover, place on a medium heat, bring to the boil and simmer for up to an hour, skimming occasionally to remove any scum which rises to the top. It is advisable to place the pan over half the heat source so that the scum rises only on one side. Top up the simmering stock with a little water if the level reduces to below the vegetable line. Meanwhile, cut the reserved chicken pieces into hazelnut-sized pieces.

When the stock tastes flavourful, remove from the heat and strain through a fine sieve, discarding the debris. Cool the broth, allowing any fat to rise gently to the top and then cover. Keep in the refrigerator for up to three days. Do not remove the layer of fat while it is stored as this will seal in the flavour.

Remove husk and hairs from the corn, and lay one by one flat on a chopping board. Remove the kernels by running a sharp knife along the length and place in a bowl. With the back of the knife carefully scrape the 'milk' from the remaining corn and add to the kernels.

Remove the fat from the chicken broth and discard. Pour the broth into a pan, discarding the fine debris, if any, at the bottom of the container and bring to the boil.

In a heavy-based pan heat the butter until foaming, add the bay leaves and corn and cook over a gentle heat for 3–4 minutes or until the corn has begun to soften. Add the flour and stir well, then the cubed potatoes and cook for a further 2–3 minutes, or until tender, stirring occasionally to prevent colouring. Gently pour the hot broth into the pan and bring it to the boil. Allow to simmer for a few minutes and taste for seasoning.

Just before serving stir in the cream, chicken pieces and chopped parsley. Serve with grilled herbed toasts drizzled with olive oil.

TOMATO

There is something to be said for not using British tomatoes until at least mid-summer or early autumn most years, as they really have to have felt the full heat of the sun, and have had the chance of ripening on the vine, before being carted off to market.

Of course the Italian and French tomatoes are available to us much earlier than that, usually by May, and at the restaurant and in the Production Kitchen we make full use of them as soon as we have tasted them and convinced ourselves that we are not jumping the gun.

In my favourite farmers' market in France, in the Luberon, the best tomatoes are sold by a man with one arm. In order to let you taste them before buying, he places the tomato on a wooden board with a nail sticking through it, carves it deftly and swiftly, picks the pieces up one by one with the tip of the knife and then offers it to you. I often come away from that stall with far too many tomatoes — enough to make salads and sauces for our household and more — as they are so tempting.

EACH SUMMER HOLIDAY in France during my childhood, the same classic tomato salad seemed to be found wherever we went – whether it was to a roadside café or on the table of a family meal in the countryside: ripe, juicy, bright red tomatoes, roughly sliced and scattered flat over a plain white plate, covered in equally roughly cut red onions and dressed with astringent red wine vinegar, olive oil, salt and finished with a big handful of chopped parsley.

I love this salad for its simplicity and rusticity but sometimes one wants something a little more or something just one step on.

Nectarines are normally found in the markets at the same time as tomatoes, and I am a great fan of fruits in salads. Crumble feta or ricotta over this salad, and then scatter with blossoms such as nasturtium, rocket flowers or marigold petals – whatever you are lucky enough to have in your garden.

TOMATO SALAD WITH NECTARINES AND FETA

650 g ripe tomatoes, plum, beefsteak or
  heritage variety
1 medium red onion
2 ripe nectarines
200 g feta or ricotta
2 tsp Dijon mustard

1 tbsp red wine vinegar
Salt and pepper
4 tbsp olive oil
2 tbsp roughly chopped parsley
Flower blossoms such as nasturtium,
  rocket flowers or marigold

Take 3 or 4 different types of tomatoes, chosen for their colours and shapes. Cut them in slices or wedges and scatter them over a flat serving dish. Slice the nectarines from the stone in wedges and place them in and around the tomatoes. Cut the red onion in half and then in paper thin slices across, making half rings. Sprinkle this on top and add shavings of feta or crumbled ricotta.

Place the mustard, red wine vinegar, salt and pepper in a bowl and whisk with a fork until blended. Gradually add the olive oil until it is to your taste. Spoon this dressing over and around the salad and scatter with the chopped parsley. Finish with beautiful blossoms if you have any and eat as soon as possible.

BAKED TOMATOES WITH GARLIC AND HERB CRUMBS

6 medium-large ripe tomatoes,
  preferably beefsteak or the ribbed
  variety
6 slices day-old bread
4 tbsp olive oil, plus a little for baking

2 cloves garlic, crushed to a cream
1 tbsp chopped marjoram
1 tbsp chopped parsley
Salt and pepper
2 tsp chopped thyme

Choose equally sized ripe tomatoes, of any shape but the heirloom varieties are best.

Place the day-old bread in a food processor and process until medium fine. This should result in approximately 160 g crumbs.

In a heavy-based pan, heat the olive oil and fry the crumbs until golden and almost crisp, stirring continuously as they will easily burn. Off the heat, add the garlic, marjoram, parsley, salt and pepper and stir well together.

PREHEAT THE OVEN TO 170°C

Slice the tomatoes in half across the equator and score deeply, in a criss-cross fashion without cutting the skin. Place them tightly together in an ovenproof serving dish, ideally terracotta, and season with salt, pepper and chopped thyme.

Place a spoonful of herbed crumbs over each tomato, drizzle with a little extra olive oil and bake for 30–40 minutes or until the tomatoes have started to collapse and the crumbs are toasted. If the crumbs start to darken before the tomatoes are ready, place a sheet of aluminium foil over and continue to cook until done. Serve from the baking dish – they are best eaten at room temperature or chilled, accompanied by a salad of leaves and herbs, tossed with red wine vinegar and olive oil.

TOMATO SAUCE WITH BASIL
AND CHILLI

1 kg ripe plum tomatoes
80 ml olive oil
1 medium onion, finely chopped
2 cloves garlic, crushed to a cream

1 tsp finely chopped rosemary
½-1 chilli, finely chopped
½ tsp salt
1 small bunch basil leaves

With a small knife remove the small cores of the tomatoes and blanch in boiling water for 5–10 seconds or until the skins easily peel away. Immediately drain and place in iced water to arrest the cooking.

Peel, quarter and then chop the tomatoes, medium-fine, retaining all the juices. Save the skins for another use such as soup or stock.

In a heavy-based pan heat the olive oil and fry the onion, garlic, rosemary and chilli until soft, then add the tomato pulp and salt and simmer for 15–20 minutes. With a sharp knife, shred the basil leaves and add to the sauce. Continue to cook for a few minutes until the sauce is soft and flavourful.

Toss into freshly cooked pasta or gnocchi, or serve as a sauce for grilled meats or fish. Alternatively when chilled, spoon onto grilled slices of ciabatta or baguette and serve either with a glass of wine before a meal or with a salad of leaves tossed with balsamic vinegar and olive oil.

Thankyou to al
our Chez Panis
was a great su
+ we are still c
the F for don
to the ESYP
STAY TUNED

FAY
MASCHER
says
sublime
goat cheese
+ gruyere
souffle!

THANK YOUS

Thirty years – half my life – have for the most part been dedicated to my work and life at the restaurant, the shop which was born out of it after just five years, and the Wholesale Bakery, its younger sibling.

Within the past two years yet another branch to the family has emerged – the Production Kitchen in North Kensington.

From one little idea, that of opening our doors to serve a small selection of daily changing dishes, and at dinner, serving just one no-choice menu, the business has grown into what we have now.

Among the individuals who have helped shape Clarke's along the way are some extraordinarily dedicated and talented people, some of whom still work alongside me on a daily basis. Others have moved on to create ventures of their own, and some, who for various reasons whilst no longer working with us, will always be part of Clarke's, no matter how far they have travelled, or how long ago they said their goodbyes. I could not have gone as far as I have, or lasted as long, without the support, hard work and focus of these special people. Continuing huge thanks go out to you all.

Sarah Bilney	Julia Devlin	Anton Loxha
Diane Bosdorf	Sarah Dickinson	Gilles Martin
David Conlon	Michelle Hattee	Phillippa O'Hara
Barry Deady	Jane Heelas	Jane Rawson

A handful of special people, who are still part of the 2015 family, have been with me for over half their own years also, and I am constantly reminding myself how fortunate Clarke's is to have them as part of its life. They are listed here, along with others who play important roles in the day-to-day operations. I am grateful to them all for their dedication and loyalty.

Paul Baldwin	Piotr Filipek	Gabriele Marzo
José Barros	Russell Henderson	Nexhat Meha
Alain Beugre-Joncourt	Tommy Higgins	Athene O'Neill
Dawn Butcher	Manuel Jesus	Fernando Rodriguez
Grzegorz Cubera	Colin Livingston	Marsolino Vincente
Nigel Eastmond	Adrian Maccelari	Sebastien William

I wonder how many people can claim to have benefited from the love and dedication of someone, now in their mid-eighties, who for over 30 years has worked with them tirelessly. Someone who has relished the idea of waking at 3.30am each Monday, to drive from the country to Covent Garden Flower Market, then on to work for a few extra hours arranging flowers and plants for the restaurant dining rooms and bar room – and to have done all this for nothing. My mother, Sheila Clarke, accomplished botanical artist, ex- (very good) amateur golfer, expert gardener, mushroom forager and grandmother to seven has been with me, in every sense of the word, since the conception of the restaurant. Along with my darling father she has supported and encouraged me, helped to paint the walls the day before opening, swept up after the builders, built table tops at home on the kitchen table, and sewed curtains to hang in the windows – all this out of love and pride for this mad daughter and her mad ideas. The restaurant would not have been the same without her. So thank you Mama for all you have done and for all you are doing.

There are two people who deserve huge thanks:

Liz Payne was my head chef for 18 years, and now lives in the York-shire Dales where she runs, with her husband and young family, a thriving bed and breakfast business, which includes a café and pro-duction kitchen (www.herriotsinhawes.co.uk). Liz worked tirelessly with me on my first book, both in the styling of the dishes for the photographs and also meticulously checking the recipes before publi-cation. Her fine attention to detail and organisational skills are beyond dispute and are amongst her most remarkable qualities. I was blessed to have her working with me for as long as I did. It took a deep breath and large gulp on my part before I picked up the phone to ask her to help again with 30 *Ingredients* – but without hesitation she agreed. So thank you Liz for being there for me – for recipe checking, testing and tasting and more! Because of this support I can, yet again, put my hand on my heart and say that the recipes work!

Rosie Dickinson, who worked with Liz and me at the restaurant in the 1990s, now runs her own organic fresh juice company from her home near Oxford (www.thehealthyjuicecompany.co.uk). She is one of those rare people who manages to meld supreme organisation with style and boundless energy who, due to her endless list-making skills, forgets nothing. She was the perfect person for me to work with on the styling of the dishes at Tessa's studio and I felt very comfortable discussing and planning each shot with her as we prepared the ingredients together.

In 1985, not long after I had opened the restaurant, Tessa Traeger photographed me for a food article in *Vogue* magazine at her studio in Chelsea. I remember arriving dressed in my clean kitchen whites, with a bowl of fermenting bread dough which would serve as the prop. I was both nervous and self-conscious, knowing how esteemed this grande dame of the camera was. She nevertheless made me feel welcome and at ease and the resulting photograph was lovely.

15 years later, she published a book, entitled *Voices of the Vivarais*, with beautiful images of landscape, nature, vegetables, fruits and the faces, hands and wrinkles of the individuals who create the foods of the terroir. Her work has a unique style and is recognisable from a glance. It has been a pleasure to have spent this time with her, and with her assistants Peter Dixon and Kate Gadsby, in the beautiful Rossetti Studios in Chelsea. Thanks also go to Sarah Wain and Jim Buckland of West Dean Gardens in Sussex, and to all at Marshford Organic Foods at Northam Bideford for their beautiful and delicious produce, and to the Conran Shop for the loan of various plates and dishes.

Enormous thanks also to designer Phil Cleaver who, very patiently, has had to deal with the erratic results of my painfully inexperienced laptop hand. His gentle and thoughtful manner has woven its way through our meetings and emails and using his skill and eye for detail, has created harmony between text and photographs. These qualities have resulted in a piece of art, of which I am now very proud.

Why Jill Norman agreed to oversee the correcting of my grammatical errors, typos and shoddily-written recipe drafts is still beyond my comprehension. But to my enormous relief, agree she did and, as with my last book, held my hand through thick and thin, with a necessary firmness from time to time, but throughout with a kindness and a gentle smile which are her trademarks. Her daughter Sasha Roth worked with her on the editing process and together they made the perfect combination for me to liaise with – professional, always in a timely fashion and all without fuss or frills. This is undoubtedly a great mother and daughter team and I was blessed to have had their encouragement and guidance throughout.

Another dream team – Toby Treves, (who often responds to emails as early as 6am), Simon Rendall (who works well into the early hours of the morning) and wonderful Katie Barkes have all gone further, and in more detail than I could ever have imagined was possible. Without them this book could not have been completed. Their patience with me has been extraordinary, always showing a kind diplomacy, with a stern word when necessary, all of which has made working through this project even more special.

And finally, which restaurant in the world could manage the day to day running of logistics, staff issues and customers' likes and dislikes without their trusted and invaluable suppliers? None of us could. Some of our best friends in the business are our suppliers, many of whom work through the night to bring us our wonderful ingredients. We raise a huge glass to you all in thanks.

Rushton Scranage, New Covent Garden

Marcus Groenendijk, The Fish Shop, w8

Adam Heanen, HG Walter w6

Rodney Macken, Macken Brothers w14

Rhug Organic Estate, Denbighshire

Johnson and Swarbrick, Lancashire

Henderson Seafood, Devon

Neal's Yard Dairy

The Ham and Cheese Company

Monmouth Coffee Company

Brian Page, Simply Garlic

Adrian Maccelari and Clarke's Bakery

Athene O'Neill and Clarke's Production Kitchen

Kate Dafter, Portobello Wholefoods, w11

INDEX

Page references for recipe
photographs are in green

blood oranges 173
blood orange ice cream with candied orange peel 177
chocolate-dipped blood oranges 174, 175–6
salad of blood oranges, beetroot and pomegranate 179, 180, 181
see also oranges
borlotti beans: leek, white bean and ham soup 144, 145
bread:
iron bark pumpkin, rosemary and pumpkin seed focaccia 250, 251–2
smoked aubergine with home-made pitta bread 40–1
spiced seeded flat bread 128
see also sandwiches; toast
breadcrumbs:
baked chicory in cream with garlic breadcrumbs 94
baked tomatoes with garlic and herb crumbs 276
dried breadcrumbs 139
broad beans 67
broad bean crostini with lemon, olive oil and ricotta 68
cracked wheat salad with broad beans, courgettes and peas 69–70
papardelle with broad beans, crisp ham and young spinach 71, 72, 73
buttermilk: warm buttermilk pancakes with poached black cherries and cream 88–9

C

cakes:
candied peel and almond macaroons 178
clementine zest madeleines 99, 100, 101
dark chocolate soufflé cake

with Kirsch and cherries 82, 83–4
pine nut and hazelnut macaroons 200, 201
Campari, clementine and vanilla sorbet 99, 100, 101
candied citrus peel 160, 161, 162
blood orange ice cream with candied orange peel 177
candied peel and almond macaroons 178
cannellini beans: leek, white bean and ham soup 144, 145
cannoli: strawberry 'cannoli' 260, 261–2
capers:
black olive tapenade toasts with anchovy and capers 170, 171
rocket salsa verde with capers and chopped egg 233
caponata 45, 46, 47
carrots:
baked beetroot and carrots with new season garlic 63, 64, 65
beetroot with potatoes, turnips, carrots and peas 60, 61–2
ceps 75
finely sliced ceps with Parmesan, lemon, olive oil and parsley toasts 76
open cep omelette with thyme and crème fraîche 78, 79
puff pastry galette with ceps, roasted onion and goat cheese 77
ceviche: scallop ceviche with landcress, lime and chilli 136, 137
Cheddar cheese: landcress and lemon mayonnaise sandwiches with nasturtium blossoms 140
cheese:
chicory salad with apple, walnuts and blue cheese 92, 93

landcress and lemon mayonnaise sandwiches with nasturtium blossoms 140
see also individual cheeses
cherries 81
dark chocolate soufflé cake with Kirsch and cherries 82, 83–4
pickled cherries with cinnamon and allspice 85, 86, 87
warm buttermilk pancakes with poached black cherries and cream 88–9
chicken:
chicken and sweetcorn soup 270–1
roasted chicken with basil 50, 51–2
chickpeas: spiced pumpkin, tomato and chickpea stew 247, 248, 249
chicory 91
baked chicory in cream with garlic breadcrumbs 94
chicory salad with apple, walnuts and blue cheese 92, 93
chicory tarte Tatin 95
chillies:
crab cakes with landcress, chilli, crème fraîche and lime 138–9
scallop ceviche with landcress, lime and chilli 136, 137
tomato sauce with basil and chilli 277
chives:
asparagus fritters with lemon slices and chive mayonnaise 32–3
figs with balsamic vinegar, chive blossoms and shaved Parmesan 129
leek vinaigrette with chopped egg, chives and mustard dressing 146, 147
chocolate:
chocolate-dipped blood oranges 174, 175–6

Frances Lincoln Limited
74 – 77 White Lion Street
London N 1 9 PF
www.franceslincoln.com

British Library Cataloguing-in-Publication Data
A catalogue record for this book is available from
the British Library

ISBN 9780711237520

Designed by et al design consultants
Typeset in Monotype Joanna
Edited by Jill Norman and Sasha Roth
Production supervision by Martin Lee Associates
Printed by Verona Libri